Baseball Bloopers & Other Curious Incidents

Baseball Bloopers & Other Curious Incidents

Robert Obojski

Sterling Publishing Co., Inc.   New York

Library of Congress Cataloging-in-Publication Data

Obojski, Robert.
  Baseball bloopers & other curious incidents / Robert Obojski.
      p.   cm.
  Includes index.
  Summary: Presents true stories of events on and off the baseball
field, with sidelights about players, managers, rules, and unusual
customs connected with the sport.
  ISBN 0-8069-6982-2
  1. Baseball—Miscellanea—Juvenile literature. [1. Baseball—
Miscellanea.] I. Title. II. Title: Baseball bloopers and other
curious incidents.
GV867.5.O36   1989
796.3570207—dc19
                                                              89-31270
                                                                  CIP
                                                                   AC

1 3 5 7 9 10 8 6 4 2

Copyright © 1989 by Robert Obojski
Published by Sterling Publishing Co., Inc.
387 Park Avenue South, New York, N.Y. 10016
Distributed in Canada by Oak Tree Press Ltd.
% Canadian Manda Group, P.O. Box 920, Station U
Toronto, Ontario, Canada M8Z 5P9
Distributed in Great Britain and Europe by Cassell PLC
Artillery House, Artillery Row, London SW1P 1RT, England
Distributed in Australia by Capricorn Ltd.
P.O. Box 665, Lane Cove, NSW 2066
Manufactured in the United States of America
All rights reserved

Sterling ISBN 0-8069-6982-2 Trade

TABLE OF CONTENTS

Fisk Hits for Second Record in One Day
Walter Alston, Home Run Slugger

5. Fun and Ballgames 70

"How Can *You* Tell Dizzy How to Pitch?"
Freak Injury in All-Star Game Dooms Dizzy
      Dean's Big League Career
Dizzy Dean, Baseball Broadcaster, Mangled
      the King's English
The Sparrow in Casey's Cap
Rookie Mantle Insults Casey
Cobb's Day
Riding on a Train with the Babe Can Be
      Dangerous
Al Simmons' "Foot-in-the-Bucket" Stance
Inaugural Game in Pacific Coast League, 1903

6. Pitchers Know It All 92

Lefty Grove's Temper Is as Famous as His
      Pitching Prowess
Rookie Refuses To Be Intimidated by Pitcher
Hubbell's Screwball "Shortens" His Career

7. Baseball Is Everywhere 100

3.6 Million Fans in the Stands?
George Will, Cub Fan
All-Star Day in the Furnace in K.C.
Even Hotter in St. Louis for the 1966 All-Star
      Game
George Bush, Good Glove, Weak Bat at Yale
The Russians Take Up Baseball
Chewing Tobacco, Anyone?
Los Angeles Dodgers Raise Oranges
At Least Somebody Came Out to the
      Ballgame!

ABOUT THE AUTHOR

Robert Obojski as a youth was an inveterate sandlot baseball player and worked his way through college by handling a number of part-time jobs with the Cleveland Indians—as a member of the grounds crew first, then operator of the electric scoreboard, and eventually as statistician for the baseball telecasts.

In the late 1950s, Obojski coached the Detroit Institute of Technology varsity baseball team and has often said since then: "Managing a baseball team, amateur or professional, is one of the most difficult and complex jobs in sport."

Over the years he has written hundreds of articles on all phases of baseball, in addition to five full-length books: *Bush League—A History of Minor League Baseball* (Macmillan, 1975), *The Rise of Japanese Baseball Power* (Chilton, 1975), *All-Star Baseball Since 1933* (Stein & Day, 1980), *Baseball's Strangest Moments* (Sterling, 1988), and *Great Moments of the Playoffs & World Series* (Sterling, 1988).

Obojski is also a well-known hobby writer, being credited with a number of books on numismatics and philately, including: *Ships and Explorers on Coins* (Sterling, 1970), *An Introduction to Stamp Collecting* (Dover, 1984), *Coin Collector's Price Guide* (Sterling, 1986), *Stamp Collector's Price Guide* (Sterling, 1986); and co-author of an *Illustrated Encyclopedia of World Coins* (Doubleday, 1970; rev. ed., 1983).

He currently serves as a contributing editor to a variety of magazines, including *Collector Editions Quarterly, Miniature Collector, Dolls Magazine,* and *Teddy Bear Review.* He is also a contributing editor to the *Guinness Book of World Records* and the *Guinness Sports Record Book,* and is a regular contributor to *Sports Collectors Digest* and *Baseball Card News.*

DEDICATION

This small volume is dedicated to Professors Lyon N. Richardson, Jacob C. Meyer and Dean Carl F. Wittke, all late of Case Western Reserve University, Cleveland, Ohio . . . three men who put up with this writer during his seven undergraduate and graduate years at that institution of higher learning.

There was no one better than Lyon Richardson in teaching students methods of research. He was an absolute fanatic about accuracy and would stop at almost nothing in tracking down loose bits of necessary information. We hope some of "Rich's" teaching has rubbed off on us.

With the United States becoming so technologically oriented, and with the work week being scaled down so dramatically, our main social problem may well revolve around this question: "What will we do with all of our newly gained leisure time?" Prof. J. C. Meyer often asked rhetorically in history classes.

One answer to that question is that we certainly now have more time to go to baseball games. Attendance at professional games—both minor league and major league—has skyrocketed in recent years. Moreover, televised games have drawn audiences running into the tens of millions.

Dean Carl Wittke was a dyed-in-the-wool Cleveland Indians fan, but at the same time he admitted, "I just like to see a well-played game, no matter who wins . . . and when you go to any major league park, you're going to see a perfectly played game, no matter that there might be an error or two."

Carl Wittke, who was also a statistical buff, observed that "since 1900, the average score of a big league game has been 5 to 3. There are things in baseball that are predictable."

ACKNOWLEDGMENTS

Special acknowledgment is again due to David A. Boehm, editor-in-chief of Sterling Publishing Co., Inc., who played a major role in helping to conceive this book and getting it into final shape for production. David is in a particularly strong position to edit baseball books since he has been a dedicated fan of the diamond game for more than six decades. Moreover, his experience in editing baseball and general sports books covers a period of nearly a half-century.

My wife, Danuta, as usual, deserves more than a word of appreciation. As a professional librarian she can quickly track down elusive bits of necessary information, but more importantly she is able to put up with me when I'm in the throes of composition.

The most curious and inaccurate observation in baseball history: "Babe Ruth made a big mistake when he gave up pitching."—Tris Speaker, 1920.

○**1**○
BLOOPERS

Mickey Owen's Famous Blooper in 1941 World Series Not Really Owen's Fault, Says Henrich 48 Years Later

Brooklyn Dodgers catcher Mickey Owen entered the "Hall of Infamy" as the result of his play in Game 4 of the 1941 World Series (contested at Ebbets Field) when he allowed a ball thrown by righthander Hugh Casey for a third strike against the New York Yankees' Tommy Henrich to get past him for an error.

The Yankees, leading the Series 2 games to 1, were in the process of losing Game 4 as the Dodgers carried a 4–3 lead going into the top of the 9th inning. Hugh Casey, the big Brooklyn righthander, in his second relief role in 2 days, retired two Yankees to start the inning. Victory seemed to be at hand for the Dodgers as Henrich came up to the plate. With the count one ball and two strikes, Casey threw a sweeping curve, missing the plate by more than a foot. Henrich swung at it, however, and that strikeout should have ended the inning and the game. BUT hold on! . . . catcher Mickey let the third strike get away from him. Henrich, on the alert, dashed off and reached first safely as the ball rolled toward the backstop.

What happened next is "history." Joe DiMaggio, always tough in the clutch, followed with a single and Charlie Keller proceeded to line a 2-run double which put the Yankees ahead. After Bill Dickey walked, Joe Gordon added insult to injury when he also smashed a 2-run double to run the score to 7–4.

Yankee reliever "Fireman" Johnny Murphy, who had entered the game in the 8th, retired the Dodgers in order in the

When Tommy Henrich of the Yankees saw that Dodgers catcher Mickey Owen had allowed Hugh Casey's pitch to get away from him, after he had swung for a third strike, he raced to first base safely. It was in the 9th inning of Game Four of the 1941 World Series. The Yankees took advantage of the "blooper" to keep the inning going enroute to beating the Dodgers. Umpire Larry Goetz is watching.

bottom of the 9th to send Dodger fans home in misery, 2 games behind.

In Game 5, Ernie "Tiny" Bonham threw a 4-hitter at the Dodgers in a 3–1 victory that clinched the Series, 4 games to 1.

The Yankees had now won their 8th straight World Series, a streak dating back to 1927, while the Dodgers lost their third straight "Fall Classic," a streak dating back to 1916.

Mickey Owen was obviously the "goat" of the Series, but did he really deserve that odious label? Not according to Tommy Henrich himself. This writer interviewed Henrich, now 76, at length during the course of a January 28, 1989, baseball memorabilia show in New York where "Old Reliable", as he came to be called, appeared as a guest. Henrich acknowledged: "Owen really didn't have much of a chance to stop that ball. Hugh Casey somehow managed to throw a wide sweeping curve—one of the biggest 'benders' I ever saw in my life—that suddenly broke down and hit at least a foot in *front* of the plate. The pitch fooled me completely, and it, of course, fooled Owen as well. Even an octopus would have had a helluva time getting a glove on that ball. Owen was really a victim of circumstances and undeservedly got a bad rap."

How does Mickey Owen, now 73, view that unfortunate play of nearly a half-century ago? Observed Owen: "I played pro ball for more than 20 years and considered myself a pretty fair country catcher. My record proves it. That third strike curve from Hugh Casey was really a dandy, and if the ball had carried 24 inches or so further, I would have caught it easily. As it is, that one play made me famous, and even to this day I get more invitations for paid appearances than I have time for. Who said 'Life isn't fair'?"

Three Runners on Third?
"Daffy Dodgers" Managed It

Floyd Caves Herman, a gangling 6-foot-4-inch 200-pound outfielder–first baseman, early in his career took on "Babe" as his nickname because as a powerful lefthanded batter he reminded sportswriters and fans of Babe Ruth. After 5 years in the minors where he perfected his technique as a fence-buster who hit for a high average, Babe Herman, then 23, was brought up to the majors in 1926 by the Brooklyn Dodgers.

From the early 1920s on, the Dodgers had ranked as a perennial second division team under manager Wilbert Robinson, but they were a fun-loving bunch who became noted throughout baseball for being pranksters and practical jokers.

And Babe Herman, who had a wicked but delightful sense of humor, soon became the "Clown Prince" of the Dodgers, who came to be called the "Daffiness Boys." Herman was usually at the center of any zaniness involving the Dodgers and very quickly he established himself as a Brooklyn favorite for his penchant for being involved in the unusual and for his ability to hammer the ball. Unfortunately, he also gained the reputation of being a weak defensive outfielder and some fanciful stories were told about fly balls bouncing off his head.

The most bizarre of all incidents involving Babe Herman occurred in his rookie year, 1926, when he averaged a solid .319 and drove in 81 runs in 137 games. In a fateful mid-season game against the Boston Braves at Ebbets Field, Herman added the most unforgettable chapter to the Dodgers' history of bloopers.

With his pitcher, Dazzy Vance, on second and second baseman Chick Fewster on first with one out, Herman lined a shot to deep right-centerfield . . . the ball struck the bleacher wall, 400 feet from the plate, on the first bounce and bounded away. Vance, undecided whether the ball would be caught, hesitated between second and third. Fewster stopped after reaching second. Meanwhile, Herman, with his head down and his long

Babe Herman, the "Clown Prince" of the Brooklyn Dodgers Daffiness Boys from the late 1920s to early 1930s, was a murderous hitter with questionable fielding skills. Whether or not he was actually hit on the head by a fly ball is still being debated by baseball historians.

legs churning, rounded first and raced for second. As the ball was hit safely, Fewster had no alternative but to take off for third, and force Vance to move on. Vance stood on the base as Fewster and Herman arrived there almost simultaneously. The ball by then had been relayed from the outfield to the second baseman, who rifled it to third. Fewster and Herman were tagged out. Vance was safe on the bag but died there. The side had been retired on what should have been a triple.

This, the weirdest double play in history, could have happened only in Brooklyn, it is said. However, it didn't stop Babe Herman.

Babe Herman's Bat
Better Than His Bloopers

Babe Herman reached his absolute peak as a hitter in 1929 and 1930, when he averaged .381 and .393, respectively, though he didn't win the league batting title in either year. Nevertheless, his .393 mark still ranks as the highest batting average in Dodgers history. In that fabulous 1930 season, Babe smacked out 241 hits, including 48 doubles and 35 homers, scored 143 runs and drove in 135.

Herman "slipped" to .313 in 1931 and then was traded away to Cincinnati. Dodgers fans howled when the Babe was shipped out and many of them decided to boycott Ebbets Field games altogether.

After one year with Cincinnati, Herman was traded to the Chicago Cubs, then went to Pittsburgh, back to Cincinnati, and played a few games for Detroit in 1937 before he slid back down to the minors. In 1945, during World War II, the Babe came back to Brooklyn as a pinch-hitter to close out his career.

In 1,552 big league games played over 13 seasons, Babe Herman averaged a solid .324. An average that high is usually good enough for Hall of Fame membership, but the Babe's questionable fielding has kept him out of the baseball shrine at Cooperstown.

The number of Babe Herman outfielding stories is endless. Tom Meany, a sportswriter who saw the Babe play many times, wrote in the old New York *World-Telegram* on several occasions that Herman was in danger of being hit on the head whenever he went after a fly ball. The Babe protested vehemently to Meany and declared that if he ever was struck by a fly ball he would never show up at Ebbets Field again.

"How about getting hit on the shoulders and arms?" Meany challenged.

"Oh, no! Getting hit on the shoulders and arms don't count," Herman begged off.

Babe Herman did lead all National League outfielders in errors for three straight seasons, in 1927-29, but for his entire major league career his fielding average came out to .971, and that isn't too shabby.

What if the Designated Hitter Rule had been instituted a half-century ago? Babe Herman would have stayed in the big-leagues for at least 20 years—and his batting statistics would have been awesome.

Bill Buckner's Blooper
Belittled 1986 Red Sox

In and around Boston, witchcraft and whaling are out, but agonizing over continuous Red Sox failures is in.

Boston won the first 2 games of the 1986 World Series against the New York Mets, lost the next 2, won Game 5 and, in Game 6 at Shea Stadium, it appeared that the Red Sox would finally take their first world title since 1918.

The Bosox broke a 3–3 tie in the top of the 10th inning when they rallied twice. Dave Henderson led off the inning with a homer and then Wade Boggs drove in the second run with a double.

In the bottom of the 10th, reliever Calvin Schiraldi retired the first 2 batters, Wally Backman and Keith Hernandez, on fly balls. Boston was now within one out of winning the World Series—but Gary Carter kept the Mets' faint hopes alive when he singled. Pinch-hitter Kevin Mitchell singled, and Ray Knight, with an 0–2 count, looped a single to center, scoring Carter as Mitchell advanced to third. Bob Stanley took over for Schiraldi at this point to hold off the surging Mets.

Mookie Wilson, the first batter to face Stanley, kept fouling off pitches as he worked the count to 2–2. Stanley's 7th pitch to Wilson was wild, and Mitchell raced home to tie the score, with Knight advancing to second base. With the count now at 3–2, Wilson fouled off 2 more pitches, and, finally, on Stanley's 10th delivery, Wilson slapped a hard grounder straight to Bill Buckner at first that looked like an easy inning-ending out. Somehow the ball got through Buckner's legs, and Knight raced home on the error giving the Mets a surprising 6–5 win that deadlocked the Series.

The Mets, with their lives so fortuitously extended, won Game 7 by an 8–5 count and became World Champions for the first time since 1969.

The Red Sox had come so close, but by now the dyed-in-the-wool Boston fans had become hardened to such agonies.

Boston manager John McNamara was severely criticized by

Boston fans and sportswriters for not inserting a defensive replacement for Buckner in the late innings. For several years Buckner had been bothered by sore ankles that hampered his mobility in the field a bit. In order to protect his ankles he had become the only player in the major leagues to wear high-top spiked shoes.

McNamara's reply to his critics was: "Look, Billy Buckner played a key role in getting us into the World Series. He knocked in over 100 runs during the regular season, and—bad ankles and all—he was still an asset in the field . . . I had no thought of removing him from the game."

Buckner had, in fact, set a major league record for assists by a first baseman in a season with 184 in 1985, and in Boston's 1986 pennant year he led all A.L. initial sackers in assists with 157. In mid-season 1987, Buckner was shipped off to the California Angels, and at the start of 1989, nearing 40, he was still active.

Unfortunately, it appears that Billy Buckner will be mostly remembered for his blooper in Game 6 of the '86 World Series. Even the most talented of players can goof up in the clutch.

Veteran Pitcher Tommy John Makes Three Errors on One Play

Tens of thousands of major league ballgames have been played since 1876, with no two of them alike—and as the old axiom goes, "Anytime you go to the park there's always a chance of seeing something completely different."

Tommy John, 45-year-old southpaw pitcher for the New York Yankees, in his 25th season in the majors, made that axiom burst into life in a July 27, 1988 game at Yankee Stadium against the Milwaukee Brewers! Normally a good fielding pitcher, Tommy committed 3 errors on one play, en route to a 16–3 win for his 285th lifetime victory.

In the 4th inning, John (1) bobbled Jeffrey Leonard's slow roller to the first-base side of the mound; (2) made a wild throw past first baseman Don Mattingly, and then, as Jim Gantner, who was on base ahead of Leonard, rounded third and headed for home, John (3) cut off rightfielder Dave Winfield's throw to

Tommy John, with the Yankees in 1988, in his 25th year in the big leagues, set a modern record for pitchers by committing 3 errors on one play.

the plate and made another wild throw—over catcher Joel Skinner's head and into the back wall.

Gantner would have been nailed by Winfield's throw, and Leonard would not have scored, but for John's 3 errors. Tommy thus became the first pitcher in modern major league history (since 1900) to achieve that dubious feat. The only previous pitcher with a triple error to his "credit" was Cy Seymour of the National League's New York Giants on May 21, 1898.

John jokingly told reporters after the game: "When I fielded the ball one-handed, I threw it like I was putting the shot . . . I should have eaten it. But with a thunderstorm coming through, there were a lot of negative ions in the air and, wearing a metal cup, it just glitched my mind."

Tommy John can afford to be funny, of course, since he's been laughing at Father Time for more than a dozen years. His career was supposed to be over in 1974 when he underwent a rare tendon transplant in his left elbow. Since then he has won well over 100 games and pitched in 5 playoff series and 3 World Series.

In recent years other pitchers have undergone similar tendon transplant surgery, a procedure now generally referred to as "the Tommy John Operation." His blooper in 1988 may well have shortened his long career.

Bob Feller Simply Didn't Watch

Bob Feller of the Cleveland Indians held the New York Yankees scoreless through the first 8 innings in a 0–0 pitchers' battle in a July 1940 game at Cleveland's League Park. Red Ruffing was on the mound for the Yanks.

Then in the top of the 8th inning with 2 out and Red Rolfe on third base, Feller faced the great Joe DiMaggio. His first 2 pitches were wide and catcher Rollie Hemsley fired the ball back to Feller—a catcher's way of saying "Get the ball over the plate!" Rapid Robert's mind must have wandered temporarily for he didn't see the ball coming back at him until the last split-second, but by that time it was too late. Feller made a wild stab at the ball, and just managed to flick it with the webbing of his glove as it sailed out into centerfield. Rolfe, on the alert, raced in and scored easily from second base. Feller was charged with an error, and the game ended 1–0.

No other incident in the history of baseball can be recalled where a pitcher missed a routine throw from the catcher, and allowed the winning run to score.

Pop Fly Blooper

Arvel Odell "Sammy" Hale, a hard-hitting infielder for the Cleveland Indians in the 1930s, had an affinity for a well worn comfortable fielders' glove.

During a July 1939 game against the St. Louis Browns at Cleveland's League Park, Hale, playing second base, settled under an easy high pop fly. There were two men on and two out and the inning should have ended—if Sammy had made the catch.

Strangely enough, however, the ball dropped *through* Sammy's glove and two runs scored as a result of the error. Those two runs turned out to be the margin of victory for the Brownies.

It seems the ball dropped right through the webbing of Hale's battered old glove. The webbing was so worn out that it simply fell apart under the impact of the ball.

After the muff, Oscar Vitt, the Indians' manager, remarked in exasperation, "'Bout time to get a new glove, Sammy!"

Baseball players a generation or two ago usually hung on to their fielders' gloves for as long as possible. For one thing, they liked the feel of a well worn glove, believing they could catch balls more easily with them. Then, the glove was the only piece of equipment that players had to buy for themselves, and they wouldn't spend money for a new one until it was absolutely necessary.

Lou Boudreau, Cleveland Indians shortstop, for example, used the same glove into the early 1940s that he had used when playing college ball for the University of Illinois in 1936–37. After relying on that one glove for 7 or 8 years, Boudreau broke down and bought another.

"That old fielder's mitt was like a part of the family, but I couldn't repair it anymore and it was falling apart on me," said Boudreau.

Fans Pay, Can't See 1948 World Series

Total attendance for the 1948 World Series, which pitted the Cleveland Indians against the Boston Braves, amounted to a very lofty 358,362, still the greatest crowds on record for a 6-game Series. The Indians whipped the Braves, 4 games to 2.

The record was set primarily because Cleveland's cavernous Municipal Stadium has a seating capacity of 78,000 (the largest in baseball), and Games 3, 4 and 5 were played at Cleveland, drawing a combined paid attendance of 238,491.

For Game 5, played on Sunday, October 10, the total paid crowd came to a whopping 86,288, the biggest turnout for *any* major league game up to that point. When all the seats were filled up, there were some 8,000 people left over, who became standees and had to be accommodated behind the outfield fence.

More than 550 ushers and some 500 policemen were required to handle the crowd. (There were actually at least 90,000 persons in Cleveland Stadium that day if all the workers were counted, including ticket takers, refreshment stand workers, vendors, ground crew members, et al.).

Most amazing of all was that a sizable percentage of those 8,000 standees could not even see the game! They had no chance, because it was impossible to see *through* people packed close to a fence. But, did they complain? Typical was one fan who paid $5 for a standee ticket (a lot of money for a sports admission in those days) who said: "I don't care whether I see the game or not. . . . I brought my portable radio with me and listened to the game play-by-play, but I just wanted to be a part of the scene and hear the roar of the crowd."

Apparently most of those 8,000 standees—enough to make up half an army division—felt the same way.

Nor did it seem to matter much that the Braves hammered the Indians that day, burying them by an 11–5 count as Boston third baseman Bob Elliott led the attack with 2 homers and 4 RBIs.

"Tomorrow's another day," said one of the Indians' loyal rooters. And so it was. On the next day at Boston, the Indians edged the Braves 4–3 behind the pitching of Bob Lemon to take the World Championship.

There had been many standing-room-only crowds at Cleveland Stadium in 1948 as the Indians set an all-time annual attendance record of 2,620,627 that stood for many years. The ballpark was the place to be—and to be seen—that glorious year in Cleveland, and if you had to stand for 2 or 3 hours and not be able to see much of the game, it didn't matter! A Cleveland Stadium filled to overcapacity for a ballgame was one of the grandest sights in all of baseball.

Called in from playing the outfield for the White Sox to substitute behind the plate for a stricken arbiter, Jocko Conlan umpired his first big league game. This auspicious career start led to his becoming one of the five umpires in the Baseball Hall of Fame.

∘2∘

THE RULING CLASS

Outfielder Called In
to Substitute for Umpire!

On a hot summer afternoon late in the 1935 season during a Chicago White Sox–St. Louis Browns game at Sportsman's Park, St. Louis, home plate umpire E. T. "Red" Ormsby was overcome by the heat. No other umpire was available or on the field. What to do? John Bertrand "Jocko" Conlan, a White Sox outfielder, was a veteran who knew the rules. So he was asked to fill in on an emergency basis! Conlan, still wearing his White Sox uniform, was glad to oblige, and umpired the rest of the game. Everyone at the park was impressed with the fact that Jocko made his calls fair and square in every instance. It was the start of a brilliant umpiring career for Jocko.

"You'd never see an incident like this happen today," recalled Conlan recently. "A player in uniform calling a major league game? Baseball was a little more informal back then."

Conlan, 36 at the time he made his "debut" as an arbiter, had already spent 16 years as a player in the majors and minors, but decided right then and there that umpiring was for him. His formal apprenticeship calling balls and strikes began in 1936 in the Class A New York–Pennsylvania League. After two years in that circuit, he moved up to the American Association, and after three years of additional seasoning in the A.A. was promoted to the National League in 1941.

Conlan, for the next 24 years, ranked as one of the top umps in the game.

Jocko Conlan credits Bill Klem, "The Old Arbitrator," for promoting him to the majors. Klem, a National League umpire for 36 years (1905–40), was chief of N.L. staff after his retirement from the field and personally selected all new recruits.

"Klem taught me to never back away from a player, especially around the home plate area. Home plate is the umpire's domain and he's got to protect it," declared Conlan.

Klem in 1953 became the first umpire to gain election to baseball's Hall of Fame in Cooperstown.

Both Klem and Conlan had nemeses from the managerial ranks who gave them real trouble over the years. Klem's chief tormentor was New York Giants manager John McGraw, while Conlan had a long string of memorable confrontations with Leo Durocher. Once, during a particularly heated argument, Durocher kicked dirt on Conlan and Jocko returned the insult by kicking dirt right back at Lippy Leo.

Conlan retired from the field after the 1964 season at the age of 65, and even while in his sixties he was known for his zip and aggressiveness.

In 1974, Jocko Conlan won election to the Hall of Fame, an honor given only to six umpires in the 115-year history of the major leagues. (In addition to Klem, the others are Tom Connolly, Billy Evans, Cal Hubbard, and Al Barlick.)

Bill Guilfoile, editor of the *Baseball Hall of Fame & Museum Yearbook,* has written of Conlan: "A polka-dot bow tie, a balloon chest protector and quick grin became his trademarks; and he won the respect of the players and fans alike with his hustle, accuracy and fairness."

As he approached his 90th birthday in 1988, Jocko retained his fierce enthusiasm for the diamond game and appeared regularly at baseball card shows and conventions all across the United States. On a good weekend Conlan has been known to give out his autograph 2,000 and more times. He'll sign anything: photographs, autograph books, baseballs, bats, jerseys, arm casts, etc., at $10 a crack.

"I've finally figured out a way to make a little bit of money out of baseball," quipped Jocko.

Umpiring Is Dangerous in Japan

Umpiring in the Oriental big leagues is perhaps what American baseball men criticize most sharply. If you think umpires take a lot of flack in America, you should see what they go through in Japan.

"Umpires in Japan don't really control the game as tightly as umpires do in the States, and there's a great deal of trouble as a consequence," observed Jim Lefebvre, who played for Tokyo's Lotte Orions in the 1970s, and who is now managing the Seattle Mariners.

In the U.S., umpires rarely change their decisions. In Japan they frequently do, sometimes two or three times before holding fast.

George Altman, a National League outfielder in the 1960s, who went on to play for the Lotte Orions for nearly a decade, recalls one game that was held up for more than an hour while the umpires debated whether an Orion batter had interfered with an opposing player trying to reach first base. The umpires kept switching their ruling, depending on which manager was arguing loudest and strongest. The debate ended only after the Orions' manager finally acceded to the umpires' fervent plea that he allow his batter to be called out.

A second base umpire changed his ruling twice before a packed house at Tokyo's Korakuen Stadium and the resultant bitter dispute delayed the game for nearly 45 minutes. "If umpires in Japan would only learn to stand their ground after making calls on close plays, there would be a lot less trouble all around," observed Jim Hicks, a veteran of both the U.S. and Japanese big leagues.

All too frequently, umpires are physically attacked by players in Japan. "Thumping the ump" has been an almost regular occurrence. In the U.S., a player could be suspended for the season or barred from baseball for life for attacking an umpire, but in Japan the offender usually draws a light fine or a brief suspension.

George Altman particularly remembers one game when he was filling in temporarily at first base for the Orions; he registered a mild protest after the umpires had called a batter safe and Altman thought he was out. "Before I could say more than a couple of words, our second baseman came over and shoved the ump about three or four feet. Then the catcher, shortstop and rightfielder arrived, and someone really unloaded, knocking the ump to the ground," Altman said.

"The ump was only a little guy," added Altman. "And I was beginning to feel sorry for him when our manager finally arrived from the dugout. I thought he would break up the skirmish, but he started shoving the umpire with the rest of the bunch!"

Joe Lutz, a veteran of more than 20 years in U.S. organized baseball, in 1975 became the first American to manage a Japanese team when he took the reins of the Hiroshima Toyo Carp in the Central League. Lutz, who had gained the respect of the Japanese baseball establishment, seemed on his way toward a long tenure as the Carp's manager, but he didn't last half the season.

It seemed that during a game in June, there was a close play at the plate and the umpire changed his decision *three times* before making a final call to the disfavor of the Carp. Lutz quit his job right on the spot and grabbed a plane back to the U.S. the very next day, never to return.

Mercifully, it appears that in recent years the Japanese have been sending better trained umpires out onto the field.

Ejected Once by Each of 17 Umpires

The argumentative Bobby Valentine, who has managed the Texas Rangers since 1985, has been ejected 17 times in his career for arguing—by 17 different umpires. Valentine certainly doesn't believe in playing favorites.

The Day an Umpire Cried

Game 5 of the 1956 World Series between the New York Yankees and Brooklyn Dodgers, long-time arch-rivals, drew a near sell-out crowd of 64,519 fans at Yankee Stadium. The Series was knotted at 2 games each and the Yankees were anxious to atone for their loss in the 1955 post-season classic to the Dodgers.

Don Larsen, one of the victims in the Yankees' loss in Game 2, took the mound against the Dodgers' Sal Maglie. Larsen, a big 6-foot-4-inch righthander, had gotten himself into the Yankee doghouse in spring training in Florida when he rammed his car into a tree after a late-evening bar-hopping session. Larsen redeemed himself over the course of the season by posting an 11–5 mark as a spot starter.

The home plate umpire for this crucial game was Ralph "Babe" Pinelli, 61 years old; after the Series' conclusion he was scheduled to retire as a National League arbiter following two decades of service. Before he took up calling balls and strikes, Pinelli had been a professional ballplayer for 15 years, spending 8 seasons in the majors as an infielder.

The fans at Yankee Stadium began going into a frenzy for they realized that through 8 innings Larsen had allowed neither a hit nor a runner to reach first base. Now in the 9th he retired the first batter, Carl Furillo, on a fly ball to right. After Roy Campanella grounded out to second, Manager Walter Alston sent his best pinch-hitter, lefthanded Dale Mitchell to bat for pitcher Maglie. Then, with the count 1 ball and 2 strikes, Mitchell took a called third strike as the Stadium exploded with a deafening roar.

Don Larsen had become the first pitcher in the 53-year history of the World Series to throw a no-hitter.

Larsen and the Yankees were happy, but Babe Pinelli was extremely disappointed. Not one of the Yankee players, nor the manager nor coaches nor Larsen, had come up to him after the game to thank him for *his* perfect performance. Later, Pinelli broke down and cried. He said, "Hell, there was a lot of pressure on Larsen, but look at the pressure there was on *me*. I had to call the balls and strikes! Just look back . . . neither of the teams put up an argument over my calls at any time during the game. Umpires never get the credit they deserve."

This was also Dale Mitchell's final game as a big leaguer, after an 11-year career in the majors, spent mostly with Cleveland. Mitchell, a .312 lifetime hitter, never argued the called third strike because he knew the pitch was within the strike zone. Mitchell commented later: "Here I average better than .300 for a career, get more than 200 hits in a season twice, play on three pennant winners, and all people remember me for now is that I took a called third strike to give Don Larsen his perfect game in the World Series."

Manush Conserves Energy, Lengthens Career

Back a couple of generations ago, major league baseball was conducted on a less formal basis than nowadays and Henry Emmett ("Heinie") Manush, a hard-hitting outfielder, seemed to exemplify that laid-back style.

Toward the mid-1930s, Manush, already a grizzled veteran then wearing the uniform of the Washington Senators (he had broken into the majors with Detroit in 1923 and won the A.L. batting crown as a Tiger in 1926 with a fat .378 mark) made it a point of conserving his energy during the "dog days" of summer.

For example, whenever the Senators rolled into Cleveland to play the Indians at League Park, Manush, a leftfielder, found a way of saving hundreds of steps each game.

After the Indians would finish in their half of an inning at bat, if Manush wasn't scheduled to bat in the Senators' half—unless there was a rally—he never walked from his leftfield post back to the visitors' third base dugout. He simply walked over to the leftfield bleachers directly in back of him, opened a little wire gate, sat himself down on a wooden bench and relaxed in the company of ticket-paying fans until the Indians were ready to bat again, and he had to resume his position in the outfield.

"Why the hell should I walk 200-some feet to the dugout when the bleachers are right in back of me?" Manush once told a reporter.

Manush's "energy conservation" tactics paid off handsomely because he lasted 25 years as a professional player (17 seasons in the majors, lifetime batting average .330) and gained election to baseball's Hall of Fame in 1964.

In and Out of One Game, Verdi Gets into Record Book

Though he was only 27 years old, Brooklyn-born infielder Frank Verdi had already spent nearly a decade in the minors—and now during the middle of the 1953 season, the New York Yankees were giving him his first shot at the majors by calling him up from Syracuse of the International League.

The Yankees, shooting for their fifth straight World Series title under manager Casey Stengel, had suddenly run short of infielders because of a rash of injuries, and Verdi was considered to be equally adept at second base and shortstop.

But he sat on the Yankees' bench for more than a week. Finally, the righthanded-hitting Verdi got his chance to get into a game when Stengel called on him to bat against a lefty St. Louis Browns pitcher in a clash at Yankee Stadium. However, when Browns manager Marty Marion saw Verdi coming up to the plate, he yanked his southpaw pitcher in favor of a righty. Casey countered by sending in a lefthanded hitter to bat for Verdi. So Verdi never batted, but he still gained credit in the record books for "appearing" in a game.

After another week or so of languishing on the Yankee bench, Verdi was shipped back down to Syracuse to finish out the season. While the unfortunate Verdi spent several more years playing in the minors, he never again saw action in a big league game.

Once his playing days were over, Frank Verdi remained in baseball as a minor league manager, and during the 1970s and early 1980s, he ranked as one of the top pilots in the New York Mets farm system, for a long period managing their Number One farm club at Tidewater in the International League. For a time Verdi also piloted the Yankees' top farm club at Columbus in the I.L.

Verdi recently commented: "Now, if Stengel had allowed me to bat in that game against the Browns, and if I had slammed out an extra base hit in the clutch . . . well, who knows how things would have turned out for me? But at least I can say that I once 'appeared' in a game for the Yankees."

Davey Johnson (left) played second base for the Orioles under Manager Earl Weaver (right), long before becoming manager of the NY Mets. Johnson, always statistical-minded, tried to convince Weaver of the value of computerized information without any success.

(Johnson photo courtesy NY Mets)

36

∘**3**∘

THE BRAIN TRUST

Davey Johnson's Printouts Don't Impress Earl Weaver

Davey Johnson, as a clutch-hitting, smooth-fielding second baseman, acted as one of the spark plugs that helped Manager Earl Weaver make the Baltimore Orioles into one of baseball's top teams of the late 1960s and early 1970s. Under Weaver, Johnson played on three straight American League pennant winners (1969–71).

Davey had a definite academic bent, especially in the field of computer technology. He attended Texas A & M University, received a bachelor of science degree in mathematics from Trinity University, San Antonio, and took a series of computer courses at Johns Hopkins University, Baltimore, during the off-season.

Weaver, on the other hand, was almost strictly a baseball man. He began playing professionally as a 17-year-old straight out of high school, worked during the off-season as a hod carrier, and began managing in the minors by the time he was in his mid-twenties.

During the course of the 1972 season when the Orioles were floundering a bit (they wound up the year in third place), Johnson prepared an elaborate series of computer printouts that analyzed the strengths and weaknesses of opposing pitchers and batters. The 29-year-old infielder strongly believed that these computer analyses would help Weaver in developing strategies against all American League teams, especially against the contenders—the Oakland Athletics, Detroit Tigers and New York Yankees.

As Johnson proudly strode into Weaver's office, he announced with obvious enthusiasm in his voice, "Skip, I really think the info in these computer printouts will give us an edge in every game we play."

Weaver, hardly looking up, grabbed the printouts, grumped out an unintelligible remark, and as soon as Johnson left the office, threw the whole batch of stuff straight into the trash can. "What the hell do I need all this mumbo jumbo for?" huffed Weaver.

As manager of the New York Mets since 1984, Johnson has won two pennants and one World Series title (he's never finished below second place)—and in the process he has utilized computer analyses liberally.

Toward the late 1970s, Earl Weaver himself is said to have begun to utilize computer-generated intelligence. "Well, I guess you've got to keep up with this modern malarkey to stay alive," Weaver reluctantly admitted.

Bo Jackson and Strikeouts

You knew that "Bo" Jackson was the 1985 Heisman Trophy winner from Auburn University. You knew that he broke all sorts of collegiate football records as a running back. And that in 1987 he began a successful pro grid career with the National Football League's Oakland Raiders. But did you know that in his first 21 at-bats for Auburn, Jackson not only failed to get a base hit, but struck out every time he came up? Nevertheless, professional baseball scouts felt that Jackson had all the necessary ability to become a diamond star. He proved them right by eventually becoming a reliable longball hitter for the Kansas City Royals, even though he's still maintaining a high strikeout average.

Ted Williams Could Smell Better Than He Could See

Ted Williams, the great Boston Red Sox slugger (who averaged .344 over a 19-year big league career) was long noted for having particularly keen eyesight. One sportswriter went overboard when he claimed that Williams followed a pitch so closely that he could actually see the ball hit the bat.

In a recent interview Williams disagreed: "No one can ever see the ball hit the bat because it's physically impossible to focus your eyes that way. However, when I hit the ball especially hard, I could smell the leather start to burn as it struck the wooden bat!"

By mid-season 1946, Ted Williams was hitting nearly .400 and everyone in the American League was thinking of ways to throttle him. For starters, Lou Boudreau, Cleveland's crafty manager, introduced the "Williams Shift" where exactly 6 fielders were stationed to the rightfield side of second base: first and second basemen and rightfielder, of course, and also shortstop, centerfielder and third baseman. It didn't help.

Birdie Tebbetts, Detroit's catcher, thought he had a better idea. While crouching behind the plate one hot summer day at Briggs Stadium when Williams was at bat, Tebbetts let loose with a torrent of words as he began to relate a long and convoluted joke in order to break the "Splendid Splinter's" concentration.

Williams, who appeared to be listening intently, let the first pitch go by for a called strike. Then the second pitch flew by for another called strike.

Finally, Williams collected himself and slammed the third pitch for a homer deep into the second deck of the rightfield stands more than 400 feet away.

After Williams loped around the bases and was about to touch home plate, he asked Tebbetts, "What was the punch line to that joke?"

Williams and Ruth—
Walks and Strikeouts

Ted Williams in 1941 enjoyed a banner year as he swatted a fat .406, going 185 for 456—and that's the last time a major leaguer reached the .400 mark for a full season.

Williams put together the rare combination of hitting with power for average, as he rapped out 73 extra base hits (33 doubles, 3 triples and 37 homers). Pitchers feared "The Splendid Splinter," walking him 145 times, giving Williams a fantastic on-base percentage of better than .550.

More remarkably, Ted struck out only 27 times, and thus he established an all-time record of walking 118 times more than he fanned. In 1942, Williams again walked 145 times, though his strikeout total increased to 51.

Before the great lefthanded slugger was through, however, he put together four more seasons in which he walked 100 or more times than he fanned. Those seasons are: (walks given first) (1946) 156, 44, plus 112; (1947) 162, 47, plus 115; (1949) 162, 48, plus 114; and (1954) 136, 32, plus 104. In 1951, Ted just missed the 100 more walks than strikeouts standard when he went 143–45.

In his 19 seasons in the majors (1939–60, with three years out for military service in World War II), Ted Williams walked 2,018 times (a figure second only to Babe Ruth's), and fanned on 709 occasions, giving him a "plus" of 1,309 in that category, far and away a big league record.

Babe Ruth received 2,056 free passes during his illustrious 22-year career (1914–35), and struck out 1,330 times, giving him an excellent "plus" of 726. Though the Babe's high mark of 1,330 K's stood as a record for a long time (Reggie Jackson now holds the all-time strikeout mark with a bloated figure of 2,497), Ruth never fanned 100 times in a single season.

Ruth reached his season high-water mark in strikeouts in 1923 when he fanned a league-leading 93 times, but he also walked 170 times, an all-time major league record. Some baseball historians estimate that at least 80 of those walks were intentional, but that figure is strictly unofficial. (Ted Williams holds the official walked-intentionally record of 33 set in 1957).

Ruth's strikeouts were almost as dramatic as his home runs. He seldom waved at a pitch when he missed it . . . he always took a full strong cut, whether he missed the ball by a foot or drove it 450 to 500 feet for a homer.

The only other major leaguer to record 100 or more walks over his strikeout figure in a single season was Eddie Stanky of the Brooklyn Dodgers. In 1945 he went 148 and 42 for a "plus" 106.

Lou Gehrig came close in 1935 when he walked 132 times and took 38 K's for a "plus" 94.

Williams Breaks Elbow, Stays in Game!

The 1950 All-Star Game, played on July 11, returned to Chicago's Comiskey Park where the interleague series had begun back in 1933.

In the first inning, Ralph Kiner (Pittsburgh Pirates) caught hold of a Vic Raschi (Yankees) fastball and lined a drive to deep left-centerfield. Ted Williams (Boston Red Sox) raced back and made a spectacular one-handed catch, but in doing so he banged hard into the wall. Despite considerable pain in his left elbow, he remained in the game until the ninth inning.

Ted, of course, didn't realize it at the time but X-rays taken the next day showed a fracture; an operation was necessary, and Ted was sidelined until early September. However, in the All-Star Game, Ted continued to roam the outfield and swing away at the plate. In the bottom of the 5th inning, Williams, broken elbow and all, smacked a sharp single to right scoring Larry Doby (Cleveland Indians) to give the A.L. a 3–2 lead. By the 9th, however, the pain became so intense that Williams asked Manager Casey Stengel to remove him from the game. The National League won the game in the 14th inning when Red Schoendienst's (St. Louis Cardinals) homer made the final score 4–3.

Ralph Kiner, now a television broadcaster for the New York Mets, commented recently on Williams' performance in the 1950 All-Star Game: "Ted robbed me of a sure extra base hit that day in Comiskey Park. He was often knocked by sportswriters for being a mediocre fielder, but when the chips were down he could be a real ball hawk. He didn't realize how serious the injury was, but through sheer grit and determination he remained in the game for eight full innings. Ted Williams was a superathlete who obviously had a very high threshold of pain."

Kiner's homer in the top of the 9th tied the score at 3–3 to send the game into extra innings.

In an Emergency, Boudreau Shines—Shortstop-Manager Fills in as Catcher

Lou Boudreau, an extremely versatile athlete, played both varsity basketball and baseball for the University of Illinois in 1936–38. In fact, he was better known as a basketball star than as a ballplayer during his collegiate days, scintillating as both a guard and forward on Illinois' famed "Whiz Kids" five of the period.

When Boudreau was called up by the Cleveland Indians in mid-season 1939 from Buffalo of the International League, he was already regarded as one of the best fielding shortstops in the game, with his sensational play. He starred for Cleveland immediately at the vital infield spot, captivating fans all over the American League.

When the managership of the Indians opened up in 1942, team owner Alva Bradley at first didn't even think of tapping Boudreau for the post until Lou made formal application. "Who can do the job better than me?" Boudreau remarked after he was hired. Boudreau, a born leader, was only 24 at the time, the youngest pilot ever in major league history. (Boudreau held forth as the Indians' player-manager for nine full seasons before moving on to the Boston Red Sox, first as a player, then as manager.)

In the sweltering heat of an August 1943 Sunday doubleheader at Cleveland's Municipal Stadium, both of Boudreau's two regular catchers, Buddy Rosar and Gene Desautels, were knocked out with injuries by the 5th inning of the second

Though Lou Boudreau was primarily noted as a shortstop he wasn't afraid to get behind the plate and catch during an emergency.

game. No other catchers were available on the entire Indians roster. What to do??

Without hesitating for a moment, Manager Boudreau himself donned the catcher's gear and handled the backstop position flawlessly for the next 4 innings. "I wouldn't ask any of my players to do what I couldn't do myself," Boudreau told reporters after the game.

"But you never caught a game in pro ball before today," injected a writer from the *Cleveland Press*.

"A *real* ballplayer can play *any* position!" Boudreau shot back.

Boudreau injected himself as an emergency backstop on two other occasions, once in 1944 and once again in 1948, the latter being the Indians' World Championship year.

In that glorious 1948 season for the Indians, Lou Boudreau, the "Flaming Frenchman," earned the distinction of becoming the first and only player-manager to win the MVP award.

The Indians and the Boston Red Sox ended the regular season in a dead heat with records of 96–58, but in a dramatic one-game playoff—the first in American League history— Boudreau paced his mates to an 8–3 victory with a 4-for-4 performance that included 2 homers.

For that 1948 season, Boudreau batted a robust .355 (second only to Ted Williams' .369) as he rapped out 199 hits, scored 116 runs and drove in 106. Incredibly, he walked 98 times and struck out on only 9 occasions in '48.

Sliding Hall-of-Famer

Mike "King" Kelly of "Slide, Kelly, Slide" fame holds the distinction of compiling the *worst* fielding average of any member of baseball's Hall of Fame (elected 1945). In 16 years in the majors (1876–93), mostly with Cincinnati, Chicago and Boston of the National League, he committed 753 errors out of 5,565 total chances, for an .865 percentage. And, Kelly, who saw service at every position, including pitching and catching, played in an era when fielders used very crude gloves or no gloves at all.

Kelly became a Hall of Famer, not for his fielding, of course, but because he was an excellent hitter (.313 average), a daring baserunner and a fierce competitor.

Getting 3,000 Hits and Batting Under .300

In the past, players who pounded out 3,000 or more base hits in their careers always wound up with lifetime batting averages well over .300. For example, Ty Cobb averaged .367 on 4,191 hits, Tris Speaker came in with a .344 mark on 3,515 hits, and Stan Musial finished at .331 on 3,630 base hits.

In recent years, however, the trend has been for players to reach the 3,000-hit milestone and average *less* than .300. Al Kaline was the first to perform the "feat." After 22 years with the Detroit Tigers (1953–74), he collected 3,007 hits but averaged only .297.

Lou Brock became the second 3,000-hit-minus-.300 man. Playing with the Chicago Cubs and St. Louis Cardinals from 1961 through 1979, Brock racked up 3,123 hits and averaged .293.

Carl Yastrzemski amassed 3,419 base hits (giving him seventh place on the all-time list) in his 23-year career with the Boston Red Sox (1961–83). Since Yaz came to bat 11,988 times officially, however, his average came to a full 15 points below .300, namely .285, and thus he went into the record books as the third 3,000-hit-minus-.300 man.

Yastrzemski had his peak years during the American League's low average era. In 1968 he led the league in batting with a .301 mark and was the only A.L. player that year (with enough times at the plate to qualify for the hitting title) to reach .300.

Oakland in 1968 led the league in batting with a puny .240, while the A.L. as a whole averaged a miserable .230. The New York Yankees brought up the year with a horrendous .214.

Robin Yount, the Milwaukee Brewers veteran centerfielder, stands the best chance of becoming baseball's fourth 3,000-hit-minus-.300 man. Through 1988, Yount at 33 and with 15 years in the majors behind him, had registered 2,407 base hits and a .290 average. Sometime in 1992, barring injury, Robin Yount should reach the 3,000-hit milestone, and unless he puts together a couple of .370–.380 seasons, he'll miss .300 by a comfortable margin.

Hall-of-Famer Fails
To Achieve .300 Batting Average

When Mickey Mantle was elected to the Hall of Fame in 1974, he had the dubious distinction of becoming the first outfielder–first baseman to enter baseball's shrine at Cooperstown, N.Y., with a lifetime batting average *below* .300. When he wound up his 18-year career with the New York Yankees in 1968, Mantle came in with a .298 batting mark, though he averaged .300 or better for 10 seasons and twice topped .350.

However, Harmon Killebrew, the former Washington Senators–Minnesota Twins long-ball hitter, had the even more dubious distinction of being the first outfielder–first baseman named to the Hall of Fame (in 1984) to go through an entire career without ever having hit .300 in any full season. (In his debut year in the majors in 1954, Killebrew did manage to go 4 for 13, .308, in 9 games.)

During his 22 years in the big leagues, Killebrew averaged only .256, the lowest of *any* Hall of Fame position player, but he more than made up for this by slamming 573 homers, the most by any American League righthanded slugger. Harmon "The Killer" Killebrew also knocked in 1,584 runs.

Yaz Never Had a 200-Hit Season

Carl Yastrzemski has the distinction of being the only one of the 14 major leaguers to achieve the 3,000-hit plateau without having had a single 200-hit season. The closest Yaz came to the 200-hit level was in 1962, his sophomore year, when he rapped out 191 safeties. He also led the A.L. in base hits in 1963 and 1967 with 183 and 189, respectively.

Yastrzemski holds the American League record for getting 100 or more hits in 22 seasons.

Al Kaline, one of the American League's leading batsmen in the
1960's, with more than 3,000 hits, had only a .297 career batting
average.

Roger Maris watches his 60th homer fly into the seats at Yankee Stadium in 1961. In the last game of that season he hit his record-breaking 61st. (NY Yankees)

Maris Hits More Than 50 Homers, Averages Lower Than .300

When Roger Maris hit his record-setting 61 home runs in 1961, the New York Yankees slugger became the first and only player in major league history to record 50 or more homers in a season and bat below .300. Maris averaged an unimpressive .269, but his astounding long ball output and league-leading 142 runs batted in gave him Most Valuable Player honors that year by a wide margin.

Roger Maris, who played in seven World Series during his 12 years in the majors from 1957 to 1968 (five with the Yankees and two with the St. Louis Cardinals), was a longtime candidate for election to Cooperstown's Hall of Fame, but most baseball experts feel that his consistently low batting average (.260 lifetime) was the primary factor that has kept him out so far.

48

A total of 10 players, including Maris, have homered 50 or more times in a single season on 17 occasions and in 16 cases the accompanying batting averages exceeded the .300 mark.

Following is a complete chronological list of the 10 super home-run hitters and the years in which the feats were accomplished, with the batting averages given parenthetically.

Babe Ruth, four times: 54, 1920 (.376); 54, 1928 (.323); 59, 1921 (.378); 60, 1927 (.356).

Hack Wilson: 56, 1930 (.356).

Jimmie Foxx, twice: 58, 1932 (.364); 50, 1938 (.349).

Hank Greenberg: 58, 1938 (.315).

Johnny Mize: 51, 1947 (.302).

Ralph Kiner, twice: 51, 1947 (.313); 54, 1949 (.310).

Willie Mays, twice: 51, 1955 (.319); 52, 1965 (.317).

Mickey Mantle, twice: 52, 1956 (.353); 54, 1961 (.317).

Roger Maris: 61, 1961 (.269).

George Foster: 52, 1977 (.320).

Most Prolific Sportswriter

Grantland Rice (1880–1954) by his own count wrote at least 74 million published words during his 53-year career as a sportswriter. In his autobiography, *The Tumult and the Shouting,* Rice says he counted in this staggering output stories and articles he wrote for newspapers, magazines and books. Thus, we can calculate that he turned out nearly 1.5 million published words per year, or nearly 30,000 every week for more than a half-century.

According to David Quentin Voight, one of the country's foremost baseball historians, Rice added new dimensions to sportswriting, especially in regard to coverage of baseball and football. Voight said: "We must remember above all that Grantland Rice was an unabashed romantic who rhapsodized over player-heroes and epochal games."

"You've Got To Have the Killer Instinct"—Reggie Jackson

"Anyone who says the World Series is 'just another game' is not a champion," declared Reggie Jackson during an interview in Oakland-Alameda County Coliseum when the Oakland Athletics and Los Angeles Dodgers were tangling in the '88 World Series. Jackson went on to say:

"The World Series is different and you must play the game different. You got to have that mental tenaciousness . . . you got to rise to the occasion . . . to put it bluntly, you've got to have the killer instinct to be a World Series hero."

Jackson, who became known as "Mr. October" for his exploits in post-season playoff and World Series competition, declared:

"I had nothing in mind in October but success. It's like Jim Brown used to say about football and like Paul Newman said in 'Cool Hand Luke,' you got to get your mind right. You can't be nice in championship play . . . you've got to be more than a little mean, you've got to be very mean."

Apparently, Jackson knows whereof he speaks, for he slammed 18 homers in post-season play, 8 in playoffs and 10 in the World Series. In one of the greatest individual performances in baseball history, Reggie, as a member of the New York Yankees, belted 3 homers against Los Angeles in the decisive Game 6 of the 1977 World Series. In that Series, Jackson hit a record total of 5 home runs, scored 10 runs and drove in 8, and personally broke the backs of the Dodgers.

Early Wynn Had the Killer Instinct

Early Wynn, who won exactly 300 games over a 23-year major league career, was noted for his actual hatred of any player who came up to home plate to face him with a bat in his hands.

"Who was the toughest hitter you ever faced?" a reporter once asked Wynn.

"Well, there were two guys," replied Wynn. "One was named Hillerich and the other was Bradsby."

(Hillerich & Bradsby is, of course, the well-known baseball bat manufacturing company based in Louisville, Kentucky.)

○4○
STARS OF FIRST MAGNITUDE

The Saga of Minnie Minoso: Five Decades in the Majors

Saturnino Orestes Arrieta "Minnie" Minoso, born on November 29, 1922 at Pefico, Matanzas, Cuba, established himself as one of the top hitters in the Cuban professional leagues in the early 1940s. A versatile and flamboyant player who could handle any position in the infield or outfield, Minnie, who stood 5 feet 11 and weighed 180 pounds, could run like a deer and drive the ball with power.

However, it wasn't until midway in the 1948 season, when he was almost 26, that Minoso got his first chance to play in the U.S. professional leagues when Bill Veeck, owner of the Cleveland Indians, signed Minnie to a contract and sent him to the Indians farm club at Dayton, Ohio, in the Class A Central League. In 11 games at the tail-end of the season, Minnie hit a stratospheric .525 (21 for 40).

Veeck promoted the "Cuban Comet" to the parent club for the start of the 1949 season and in 9 games Minoso averaged only .188 (3 for 16), but one of those base hits was a 400-foot homer into the Cleveland Stadium's rightfield stands, not a mean feat because Minnie hits righthanded. (This writer was on hand to watch Minoso in action on that day.)

Toward the end of April, the Indians farmed Minoso out to San Diego of the Pacific Coast League for "further experience," though Minnie had already played professionally for a decade. Minoso remained with San Diego through 1950 and established himself as a star in the P.C.L.—in that 1950 season he rapped out 203 base hits, scored 130 runs, batted in 115 runs and averaged .339 at the plate.

MINNIE MINOSO
CHICAGO WHITE SOX   OUTFIELD

This earned him another shot with the Indians, but through the first weeks of the 1951 season Minnie floundered with the bat as he struggled to stay over the .200 mark. Then on April 30, Cleveland traded Minnie away to the Chicago White Sox in a complicated three-team deal involving a total of seven players. (Veeck had sold off the Indians in late 1949 and was now running the St. Louis Browns.)

Immediately after Minoso joined the White Sox, he caught fire again and became the talk of the league as he hit consistently, ran the bases like a demon (led the A.L. in stolen bases with 31), and played the outfield with a reckless abandon in the style of Willie Mays. He concluded the season with a healthy .326 average and was among the league leaders with 112 runs scored.

"If it had been up to me, I would have never traded Minnie," Bill Veeck remarked at the time.

Minoso remained with the White Sox through 1957, averaging well over .300 and then was traded back to the Indians, where he remained for two seasons, hitting a solid .310 and .302.

After the 1959 season, the Indians traded Minoso back to Chicago where he put in another sterling two years as he averaged close to .300 in his second tenure with the Sox.

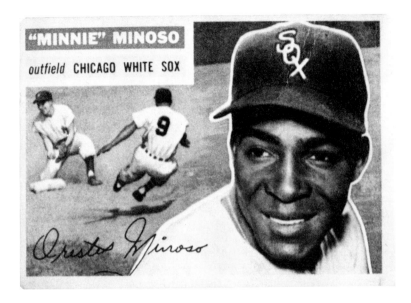

"MINNIE" MINOSO
outfield CHICAGO WHITE SOX

Orestes Minoso

Traded again in 1962, Minoso went to the St. Louis Cardinals where he was expected to be the regular leftfielder. Minnie, pushing 40 now, continued to cavort on the diamond with boyish enthusiasm, but on May 11 while chasing down a long drive, he crashed into a concrete wall at St. Louis' Sportsman's Park and suffered a skull fracture and broken right wrist. Minnie recovered, got himself placed back on the active list in late July, but was used sparingly thereafter. The Cardinals, feeling Minnie was all washed up, traded him to Washington in 1963. Minoso, well past 40 and beginning to show signs of age, hit only .229 in 109 games for the Senators and was handed his unconditional release at season's end.

The White Sox signed Minnie as a free agent at the beginning of 1964, expecting him to be their No. 1 pinch-hitter. After getting into only 30 games, Minoso was released in mid-season, but he immediately hooked on with Indianapolis of the Pacific Coast League where he played regularly as an outfielder–third baseman for the rest of the year.

"Orestes Minoso is obviously finished as a player now and should turn to coaching or managing if he wants to stay in the game," declared one New York sportswriter as the 1964 season wound down to a conclusion.

MINOSO

Orestes "Minnie" Minoso, at the age of 53, became the oldest man in major league history to get a base hit. At the age of 57, he became the oldest player to pinch-hit in the big leagues. Nearing 70, he still plays regularly in Old-Timers games.

But Minnie just said "No" to that kind of negative thinking and signed a contract with Guadalajara, Jalisco, of the Class AAA Mexican League. He proceeded to have one of the best years of his pro career as he hit a fat .360, and led the league with 106 runs and 35 doubles. And in 508 chances in the outfield he made only 11 errors.

We should also mention that Minoso continued playing a full schedule in the Caribbean Winter League, a season that lasted from about mid-October to mid-February and consisted of as many as 75 games. Minnie had started his career in the Winter Leagues back in the mid-1940s, and so with his summer seasons he averaged more than 225 games a year.

Minnie sat out a month of the 1966 season with Guadalajara because of injuries, but when he was healthy enough to play he managed to swing a potent bat, as he averaged .348 in 107 games.

His career took on a new turn in 1967 when he signed to manage Orizaba in the Class A Mexican Southeast League. Minoso, still a player at heart, was not satisfied to be a mere bench manager, so he played in about half of Orizaba's games and showed his minions how to hit as he averaged .350.

Minoso shifted over to Puerto Mexico of the Mexican Southeast as player-manager for the 1968–69 seasons and continued to hit better than .300 while dividing his time between the outfield and first base.

"I'm pushing 50 so I have to rest up a little from chasing down balls in the outfield by sticking myself at first base," Minnie said at the time.

In 1970, Minoso went back to the Class AAA Mexican when he signed up with Gomez Palacio as player-manager and for the next two years maintained his standing as one of the top hitters on the diamonds south of the border. Minnie in 1971 played in more than 100 games because of a rash of injuries incurred by his squad.

Minoso finally became tired of managing and decided to put his full energies into *playing* with Gomez Palacio, and in 1972–73 he played a full schedule at first base and hit .285 and .265, respectively, in those two seasons, good figures for an ordinary player, but sub-par for Minnie.

As the 1974 season approached, Minoso, now 51, thought it was time to retire as an active player, but in 1975, itching to get back into baseball, he signed on as non-playing manager for Leon in the Class A Mexican Center League.

In 1976, Minoso's old friend Bill Veeck began his second tenure as owner of the Chicago White Sox and in one of his first moves Veeck hired Minnie as a coach. Minnie was still in great physical condition. He had hardly strayed from his old playing weight of 180, and was hyperactive as a coach, taking regular batting and fielding practice.

Veeck, always the promoter, activated Minoso to playing status late in the '76 season as a designated hitter–pinch-hitter. Minnie was thrilled at this move and in his first game as a DH Minoso singled sharply to center. At 53, Minnie had the distinction of being the oldest man in major league history to hit safely.

(In a 3-inning pitching stint with the Kansas City Athletics in 1965 Satchel Paige, said to be 59, batted once, but he struck out. Paige stands out as the oldest man to have ever played in a regular season major league game. Charles O. Finley, then owner of the A's, had earlier signed Paige as a coach and thought old Satchel still had enough moxie to pitch effectively in the majors. Finley was right because Paige got through those 3 innings without allowing a run.)

In 3 games as a DH–pinch-hitter in '76, Minnie went 1 for 8 before retiring once again to the coaching lines. Minoso remained with the White Sox as a coach through Veeck's tenure as owner, and then late in the 1980 season, Veeck came up with another brainstorming idea to help draw crowds into Comiskey Park.

He pulled Minnie off the coaching lines once again and activated him as a pinch-hitter. The idea was to get Minoso into the record books as the only major leaguer to have played in five different decades—from the 1940s into the 1980s. Minnie went 0 for 2 in two pinch-hitting roles, and though he didn't succeed in hitting safely he went into the record books again—at 57 he became the oldest man sent into a regular season game to pinch-hit.

Veeck sold the White Sox after the '80 season, and though Minoso remained with Chicago as a coach, his playing days came to an end—except for his regular appearances in Old-Timers' games down through the rest of the 1980s. Even as he approached his late 60's, Minnie still looked every inch the ballplayer.

Over 17 major league seasons, Orestes Minoso hit a very solid .298 (1,963 hits in 6,579 official times at bat in 1,835 games), scored 1,136 times and batted in 1,023 runs—and he was always considered to be an excellent fielder. That's pretty close to Hall of Fame caliber and Minnie may yet be elected to baseball's shrine at Cooperstown.

This writer has made efforts to compile Minoso's complete professional regular season record, starting with his Cuban League play of the early 1940s, and going through his long minor league career (in both the U.S. and Mexico), together with his Caribbean Winter League stats.

Roughly, these are our findings to date: Minoso has played in well over 5,000 professional games, been to bat at least 20,000 times officially, stroked more than 6,000 base hits, including over 650 homers and maybe 1,000 doubles, and has scored and batted in over 3,500 runs. (These figues do not include exhibition games.) It's our firm belief that no other professional player can approach the magnitude of these statistics.

As Minnie Minoso told us recently: "Don't count me out as a player yet . . . I still get into at least 20 Old-Timers' games every season!"

The Curious Case of Buzz Arlett

Russell "Buzz" Arlett, a hulking 6-foot-3-inch 225-pound mass of muscle reigned as one of the Pacific Coast League's biggest stars during the 12-year period between 1919–30 as he sparkled on the pitcher's mound, at bat and in the outfield for the Oakland Oaks. As a righthanded hurler with an excellent curve and fastball, he topped the 20-victory mark in each of three seasons and then, from 1923 on, he was consigned almost primarily to outfield duty because of his potent bat.

A switch-hitter, he averaged well over .300 regularly, topped the 100 RBI mark for 8 straight years (1923–30), and in 1929, his banner year, he batted a fat .374, slammed 39 homers and knocked in 189 runs. After hitting .361 in 1930 and stroking out 270 base hits in exactly 200 games, Arlett, now 32, was finally given his first shot in the majors as the Philadelphia Phillies purchased his contract from the Oaks.

So how did Arlett do in 1931 for the Phils? Why, in 121 games he batted a potent .313 and piled up 51 extra base hits (26 doubles, 7 triples and 18 homers), good for a hefty slugging average of .538.

Nowadays an outfielder turning in that kind of stat line would be screaming for (and getting) a 3-year million-dollar contract. But how did Arlett do in his contract negotiations? Poorly . . . very poorly. He was sent back to the minors and never played another game in the majors!

While with the Baltimore Orioles of the International League in 1932, Arlett was still at the peak of his powers as he averaged .339, and led the league with 54 homers and 144 RBIs. In that '32 campaign, Arlett hit 4 homers against Reading on June 1 at Reading, and then in a July 4 game, he hit another 4 homers against Reading at Baltimore. No other player in professional baseball history has bashed 4 homers in a game twice in the same season.

Arlett continued to play into 1937, finishing his career with the Syracuse Chiefs of the I.L. Recently the Society for American Baseball Research (SABR) chose Buzz Arlett as the Greatest Minor Leaguer of all time. In 2,390 games, he picked up 2,726 base hits, averaged .341, ripped 1,037 extra base hits (598 doubles, 107 triples and 432 homers), scored 1,610 times and drove in 1,786 runs (this does not include his year with the Phils).

As a pitcher with Oakland, he went 108–93 and compiled an excellent 3.45 ERA in a heavy-hitting era.

Why Arlett did not stick with the Philadelphia Phillies beyond a single season is a question that still mystifies baseball historians. Certainly his outfielding wasn't all that bad since in 1931 he committed only 10 errors and had 14 assists, a good number for an outer gardener. But as the old axiom goes, "There are certain things about baseball that cannot be explained."

Joe D's Streak of 61

Did you know that Joe DiMaggio's record of hitting safely in 56 consecutive games was beaten? by Joe himself? Yes, in 1933 he had a streak of hitting safely in 61 consecutive games when he was an 18-year-old rookie with the San Francisco Seals in the Pacific Coast League. He kept the streak going from May 28 through July 25 by pounding out 104 hits in 257 official at-bats for a .405 average.

Joe DiMaggio in 1951 was nearing 37, not all that old, but the "Yankee Clipper" was obviously past his prime as he struggled to keep his batting average from going below the .260 mark.

Going into Cleveland's Municipal Stadium for a late July game against the very tough Cleveland Indians, Joe was still batting fourth, the "clean-up spot," but he wasn't driving in runs with his usual consistency.

Cleveland had big fireballing righthander Mike "Big Bear" Garcia on the mound to tame the Yankees, who were in first place in the American League pennant race by a slim two-game margin over the Indians.

In the top of the seventh inning, with the score tied, 1–1, Garcia got into a bit of a jam as he had a runner on second base with one out. Yankee first baseman Joe Collins, batting third, came striding up to the plate and Garcia proceeded to take an action that hitherto was considered unthinkable. He was ordered by Manager Al Lopez to walk Collins intentionally to *get at* DiMaggio. Mel Allen, broadcasting the game for the Yankees, muttered almost in disbelief, "I can't recall any

The Yankee Clipper's record of hitting in 56 games consecutively stands as one of base- ball's outstanding achievements. But Joe DiMaggio hit safely in 61 consecutive games!

pitcher intentionally walking the man preceding DiMaggio in the lineup."

Joe D himself probably winced a bit as he came to the plate. On Garcia's first delivery, however, he mistakenly threw a belt-high fastball; the Yankee Clipper connected and sent a vicious line drive that went whistling past Garcia's ear and out into centerfield for a single, scoring the man from second. No one was going to show up the great DiMaggio—and that RBI single turned out to be the game winner for the Yankees.

Nevertheless, DiMaggio knew the end was coming and other situations would probably follow where pitchers would simi- larly challenge him, and situations where the aging DiMaggio might fail to come through.

That '51 season ended successfully for the Yankees. They captured the pennant by a comfortable 5 games over the runner-up Indians and then whipped the New York Giants in the World Series 4 games to 2.

DiMaggio wound up the regular season batting .263 (the lowest average of his career by far), drove in a respectable 71 runs in 116 games, but found that he was being "rested" more and more frequently by Manager Casey Stengel. In the World Series, DiMag batted in 5 key runs and played his centerfield position flawlessly.

In December, the Yankees offered DiMaggio a second consecutive $100,000 contract for the 1952 campaign (big money in those days), but he demurred and said: "Sure, I'd like to play another year for a six-figure salary, but it wouldn't be DiMaggio out there." Thus ended the Yankee Clipper's active career.

As Rudolf Bing, the longtime Metropolitan Opera impresario, once said, "In any profession, it's better to quit too soon than too late."

Japanese Hero Unceremoniously Dumped

Japan's biggest baseball stars are generally rewarded with manager's posts at the conclusion of their active playing careers. And Sadaharu Oh, the great slugger who blasted 868 regular season homers in a 22-year career with the Central League's Tokyo Giants (1959–80), was no exception to this custom.

After serving as a coach for three years, Oh, called "The Japanese Babe Ruth," was appointed manager of the Giants. And during a five-year stretch his team never won the "Japan Series" (an affair that pits the pennant winners of the Central and Pacific leagues in a best-of-seven playoff).

Oh's Giants captured one pennant, in 1987, but lost the Japan Series to the Pacific League's Seibu Lions. After the Giants finished a "miserable" third in the six-team Central League in 1988, Oh was summarily fired, an act that sent shock waves throughout Japan. Oh's legions of fans thought he had a lifetime job as manager because of his towering hero status.

Once he was given the axe, Oh made these comments, which are reminiscent of those made by U.S. big league managers when they are fired:

"Over the past five years I have not been able to meet expectations, and I accept that. In this world of professional sports, you have to win. That's the bottom line."

The Japanese are certainly beginning to sound as if they're being Americanized!

O'Doul Gets Hits, Suffers in Depression

Frank "Lefty" O'Doul, a native of San Francisco, played in his first professional baseball game with Des Moines, Iowa, of the Western League in 1917 at the age of 20.

O'Doul started out as a pitcher, receiving trials with the New York Yankees and Boston Red Sox, and then switched to the outfield because of arm problems. From 1924 through 1927 O'Doul ranked as one of the top hitters in the Pacific Coast League, with his best year of production coming for Salt Lake City in 1925 as he rapped out 309 base hits in 198 games, averaging a cool .375.

After piling up 278 base hits in 189 games and averaging .378 for the San Francisco Seals in 1927, O'Doul was called up by the New York Giants for the following season. And so at the age of 31 Lefty O'Doul was finally in the big leagues to stay for a while.

For the next seven years he terrorized National League pitching, winning two batting crowns. He found himself in a Philadelphia Phillies uniform in 1929 and proceeded to lead the league with a .398 mark as he racked up 254 hits, still a National League record. While with Brooklyn in 1932, he paced N.L. hitters again, this time with a .368 mark.

And how was O'Doul rewarded by the Dodgers for winning a batting title? Was he given a substantial raise? Absolutely not! He was cut by $1,000, from $9,000 down to $8,000. Remember this was 1932—the midst of the Great Depression—and economy was the order of the day in regard to baseball salaries.

O'Doul concluded his big league playing career during a second tour of duty with the New York Giants in 1934 (he hit .316) and then began a long managerial career in the Coast League, starting with the San Francisco Seals in 1935.

Lefty O'Doul (he threw and batted lefthanded) kept himself on the Seals active roster as a pitcher and occasional pinch-hitter, and made his final appearance in a Seals game in 1945 as a substitute batter. Lefty was now 48.

After O'Doul left the Seals following the 1951 season, he made P.C.L. managerial stops at San Diego, Oakland, Vancouver and Seattle. While with Vancouver in 1956, Lefty inserted himself into a late season game as a pinch-hitter and delivered by smashing a booming triple that hit the fence in right-center field. O'Doul refused to take himself out of the game in favor of a pinch-runner and scored when one of his charges singled to center.

At the age of 59, Frank Joseph Lefty O'Doul had become the oldest man in the history of professional baseball to get a base hit in a regular season game.

We spoke with O'Doul about his history-making triple in the fall of 1959 at his San Francisco restaurant and bar. Lefty recalled: "The pitcher underestimated me. He apparently thought about my age at the time—nearly 60—and he threw me a fairly easy pitch to hit and I really unloaded. Since I began playing as a pro in 1917, my first and last base hits came almost 40 years apart. I don't believe any other player could make a statement like that."

Lefty O'Doul died in 1969, but he continues to be remembered as one of baseball's most colorful personalities and each year the drive to have him elected to baseball's Hall of Fame grows stronger. As a major league player, O'Doul batted a robust .349 in 11 seasons.

Moreover, he helped lay the groundwork for the creation of Japan's first professional baseball league—the Central League—in 1936. He even named Tokyo's entry in the Central League as the Tokyo "Giants" since he was playing for the New York Giants when the circuit was in the planning stages.

O'Doul visited the Orient many times, conducted numerous baseball clinics at Japanese colleges and universities, and played a major role in reactivating professional baseball in Japan immediately after the conclusion of World War II.

Frank O'Doul should gain Hall of Fame membership not only for his playing ability but for his contributions to the game as a whole.

Fancy-fielding Brooks Robinson, the best third baseman the Orioles ever had, was idolized by the Baltimore fans.

Brooksie's Fans Are Fanatics

When Baltimore Orioles third baseman Brooks Robinson was inducted into baseball's Hall of Fame at Cooperstown, New York, in the summer of 1983, forty large buses loaded down with more than 2,000 of Brooksie's fans chugged in from Baltimore for the ceremony. Never before in history had a single inductee attracted that many fans to the Hall itself. Oddly, Robinson has never attended an induction ceremony since that time, although all Hall of Famers are strongly encouraged to come to Cooperstown for that gala occasion (all expenses paid, of course).

Bobby Doerr, Boston Red Sox Hall-of-Fame second baseman, bent down so many times to pick up ground balls that he developed serious back problems and was forced to retire at 33.

Picking Up Too Many Ground Balls Can Be Dangerous to Your Health

Bobby Doerr was brought up to the majors with the Boston Red Sox in 1937—he was still only 19—and remained with the Bosox for 14 seasons (skipping the 1945 campaign when he was in the U.S. Army), playing second base exclusively.

Named the American League's Most Valuable Player in 1944, he was picked for the A.L. All-Star team.

Toward the end of the 1950 season and through 1951 Doerr

began experiencing severe back pains. Though he was forced to miss 50 games in '51 because of those back problems, he still managed to hit .289, covered his position at second base, and was named for the eighth time to the All-Star team.

As the season progressed, however, the back pains grew worse, and there were times when he had difficulty putting on his suit coat after a game. Sometimes the trainer had to help him. Finally Doerr's doctors told him he'd have to quit playing altogether if he expected to remain in good health for the rest of his life.

Doerr made these comments on his problem: "Over the years I bent down so many thousands of times to pick up ground balls that my sacroiliac went out of whack. The doctors advised me in no uncertain terms that if I didn't stop playing I'd be walking around like a hunchback. I was only 33, but, unfortunately, my playing career was finished."

Doerr was elected to the Hall of Fame in 1986.

Jim Rice, Baseball's Strong Man

Jim Rice, standing 6 feet 2 inches tall and weighing 220 pounds, for years ranked as one of the strongest men physically in the major leagues. He slammed out numerous tape-measure homers for the Red Sox, some traveling distances of 500 feet. His best year was 1978, when he hit for the circuit 46 times, and by the end of the 1988 season, Rice approached the 400-homer mark.

His awesome strength became graphically apparent one day when Rice was standing in the batter's circle taking practice swings when suddenly his bat broke in half. He had gripped the war club so tightly and swung so hard that the wood simply splintered from the force of the practice swing.

Don Zimmer, Boston Red Sox manager at the time, who viewed the incident, said: "In over 35 years of baseball, I've never seen a player break a bat that way before. Only a man with Paul Bunyan strength could do it."

"Specs" Toporcer Was First to Wear Glasses on the Field

"If a frail kid with a slight build, weak eyes and no high school or college training could jump directly from playing sandlot baseball to the big leagues—and stick for seven seasons!—then almost any young player with a passion for the game can do the same thing.

"I was that kid I'm talking about. My baseball career started when one of my grammar school teachers (in New York City) organized a team of kids. I begged for a chance, but he ignored me because I wore thick glasses and I was small and skinny. No one had ever heard of wearing glasses when you played with a 'hard ball' in those days!

"But one day only eight players (and I) showed up. The teacher-manager *had* to use me in the outfield. I made a good catch and a couple of hits. From that day on, I was 'in.'"

So begins an inspiring book, *Baseball: From Back Yard to Big League,* by George "Specs" Toporcer, published in 1954 (Sterling), long after that incident in a gravel schoolyard on the East Side of New York City.

After starring for strong semi-pro teams in Brooklyn and New Jersey in 1919–20, Toporcer was noticed by major league scouts and signed a contract with the St. Louis Cardinals, then managed by Branch Rickey. He was invited to the Cards' spring training base at Orange, Texas and made the team as a second baseman. Thus, Specs Toporcer became the first player in the major leagues other than a pitcher to wear glasses on the field.

Toporcer wrote in his book: "Rickey sent me, skinny and bespectacled as I was, out onto the field in St. Louis to open the season for the Cardinals at second base! And to top it off, Rogers Hornsby, the league's leading hitter, was shifted to third to make room for me!"

Later in that 1921 season, the 22-year-old Toporcer was farmed out to Syracuse, but he came back with the Cards in 1922 and stayed with them continuously through the first couple of weeks of the 1928 season when he was named player-captain of the Rochester Red Wings, the Cardinals' top farm club.

Toporcer's role in his seven seasons with St. Louis was mostly that of a utility infielder, with his best year being 1922 when he batted .324 in 116 games. In 1924 he hit a potent .313 in 70 games. Overall, in 546 big league games, he averaged .279 at the plate and was known as a sure-handed infielder.

He wrote further in his book: "During the 7 years I was with the Cardinals, I played next to Frankie Frisch, Grover Cleveland Alexander, Rogers Hornsby, Jim Bottomley, Billy Southworth, Chick Hafey, Ray Blades, "Pop" Haines and many others. I had ample opportunity to study how they played the game."

Specs Toporcer really hit his stride as a player with the Red Wings as he was named the league's Most Valuable Player in 1929–30. In 1929, the pennant-winning Red Wings, with second baseman Toporcer as captain leading the way, reeled off 225 double plays, a mark that has never been eclipsed in organized baseball. The Red Wing infield, which was responsible for most of the twin killings, consisted of, in addition to Toporcer: "Rip" Collins, first base; Heinie Sand, shortstop; and Joe "Poison" Brown, third base.

Toporcer went from captain of the Red Wings to become a player-manager. In 1931, he went to Jersey City of the International League in that capacity, then back to Rochester, 1932–34. "Specs" last appeared in a regular season game as player-manager with Albany, New York, of the Class A Eastern League in 1941. One of his prize pupils at Albany in that year was an 18-year-old outfielder named Ralph Kiner, later to be the major league home run slugger and member of the Hall of Fame.

Specs remained in baseball as farm director of the Boston Red Sox and served his last stint as a minor league manager with Buffalo of the International League in 1951.

Tragically, after that 1951 season, Toporcer became completely blind, but he didn't allow anything to prevent him from being active in and around the baseball scene. Doctors had performed a major operation on his eyes, yet failed to save his sight. For a number of years he traveled the U.S.A. making speeches, primarily to young people.

"He'd tell them," recalled his wife Mabel (the Toporcers marked their 66th wedding anniversary in 1988), "that no matter what happens to you, don't give up." He never had a

First fielder to wear glasses was George Toporcer, who played with the World Champion St. Louis Cardinals in the 1920's in the infield with Rogers Hornsby.

*

Seeing-Eye dog, and never needed a cane. "Mabel," he said, "has been my eyes."

Toporcer, who celebrated his 90th birthday on February 9, 1989, lives today in Huntington Station, Long Island, N.Y., and still follows the game avidly through speaking with old friends from his baseball days and through radio broadcasts. When Specs Toporcer came onto the major league diamonds in 1920 wearing glasses, he made a real stir. Nowadays, however, no one gives a second thought to a player with "four eyes." Even Reggie Jackson wore glasses for most of his long career in the majors.

Maybe one of these days we'll see an umpire wearing glasses!

* Died May 1989.

Fisk Hits for Second Record in One Day

On the evening of Friday, August 19, 1988 at Detroit, Carlton Fisk, 40-year-old Chicago White Sox catcher, broke an American League record by appearing in his 1,807th game behind the plate. (Rick Ferrell had held the old record for catchers of 1,806 games.)

Fisk celebrated the occasion by going 5-for-5, singling 4 times, tripling and driving in 2 runs. This was Fisk's first 5-hit game in his 19 years in the majors. Despite Fisk's performance the Tigers beat the White Sox that night 5–4.

"I didn't do anything differently in this game," Fisk told reporters later. "On other occasions, I've hit the ball hard 4 or 5 times and every drive went straight into an outfielder's glove. There are some things about baseball you just can't explain."

Walter Alston, Home Run Slugger

You know that Walter Alston, long-time manager of the Dodgers, played in only one game in the major leagues and had a single at-bat. (He struck out.) But did you know he was a power hitter in the Middle Atlantic League with a total of 176 circuit clouts, leading the league in homers no less than 4 times?

∘5∘

FUN AND BALLGAMES

"How Can *You* Tell Dizzy How To Pitch?"

Jay Hanna ("Dizzy") Dean, son of a poor Arkansas share-cropper, burst upon the big league scene in 1932 with the St. Louis Cardinals and the big, brash righthanded fireballer, averaged 24 victories a season over each of his first five campaigns.

Dizzy enjoyed his best season in 1934 when he posted a glittering 30–7 record to help lead the Cards to a National League pennant. Diz' younger brother Paul ("Daffy"), also a hard-throwing righthander, contributed 19 victories to the pennant drive—thus, the two Dean boys won just over half of St. Louis' 95 victories.

Most good pitchers receive instruction from coaches for long periods and painstakingly develop techniques to make them effective moundsmen. Dean, a natural athlete, however, was entirely self-taught. Dizzy, who stood 6 feet 3 inches tall and weighed about 200 pounds, possessed a pitching style that was marked by a graceful and powerful rhythm; with a majestic sweep of his arm, he let the ball fly and kept poised and alert after the pitch. Throwing a baseball never held any mysteries for him and he believed wholeheartedly—without a shadow of a doubt—that he was the greatest pitcher in the world.

On one occasion a reporter came up to Dean and asked him how he came to be a great pitcher. Diz, whose tongue was often as sharp as his fastball, replied without a moment's hesitation: "I learnt everythin' myself. . . . I jest like to rear back and fog 'em through!"

Dizzy Dean didn't take kindly to advice—he knew how to pitch.
Here he is scoring in a World Series game against Detroit. (From
"Great Moments of the Playoffs and World Series")

He relied on his great fastball to intimidate batters, and went on to lead the league in strikeouts for four straight seasons (1932–35). He set a modern National League mark for strikeouts in a single game when he fanned 17 Chicago Cubs on July 30, 1933—a record since broken by Sandy Koufax, Steve Carlton and Tom Seaver.

Dean, who maintained an absolute self-confidence as to his abilities (many players labeled him as an outright braggart), hardly concerned himself with listening to scouting reports about opposing batters. "I never bothered about what those guys could hit or couldn't hit," he once chuckled. "All I knowed is they weren't gonna get a holt of that ball Ol' Diz was throwin'."

Before a game against Boston early in the 1934 season, Dizzy loudly proclaimed to everyone within hearing distance that he wasn't going to throw a curve during the entire nine innings. He would unleash only his fastball. He didn't bend a curve all afternoon as he shut out the Braves 3–0, allowing only 3 singles.

Dean often drove his catchers batty by insisting on pitching to a hitter's strength. He never worried about playing it safe. "A great pitcher is supposed to strike 'em all out the hard way," Dizzy reasoned, and that's what he always tried to do, at least during the peak of his career.

Frankie Frisch, a grizzled veteran of the diamond wars, who came to the Cards from the Giants as a second baseman in 1927 and who took over as manager in mid-season 1933, loved Dizzy like an errant kid brother.

As Frankie went through the travails of trying to lead his team to a pennant with Dean as the ace of his pitching staff, he experienced a variety of emotions—he suffered and sweated and wept and rejoiced—sometimes all on the same day. Frisch continuously tried to tell Diz how to pitch to enemy batters but without much success. Several times, for example, old "Fordham Flash" Frankie would walk toward the mound from his second base position to offer a pitching tip, but Dean would haughtily wave him away.

Matters came to a head on September 21, 1934 when Dizzy and Paul were slated to go up against the Brooklyn Dodgers in a late-season doubleheader. In the clubhouse before the start of the twin bill, Frisch went through the Brooklyn lineup, painstakingly trying to explain to Dizzy how to "feed 'em to the hitters." Diz came out with either a grunt or a wisecrack for each tip. He finally held up his hand and broke into this instructional session with these remarks:

"Now listen here, Frankie. . . . I've won 26 games so far this season and it don't look right for no infielder to be tellin' a star like me how to pitch a game o' ball."

Frisch blew his top and looked as if he were going to belt his ace pitcher, but Dean only grinned broadly.

"Aw, now, Frankie," he countered good-naturedly. "Don't get so excited. I doubt if them Dodgers get a hit off'n me or Paul this afternoon."

Dizzy happened to be in top form that day and held Brooklyn hitless through the first 7 innings. With two out in the 8th, the Dodgers got their first hit of the game and Dean had to settle for a 3-hit shutout. Then Paul took over in the next game and, amazingly enough, threw a no-hitter!

Dizzy, who was clearly upstaged by his brother, told reporters: "I wish I'd a known he was goin' to pitch a no-hitter today. I would of, too."

After this memorable day, Frankie Frisch rarely offered any pitching advice to either of the Deans.

The Dean brothers went on to become even bigger heroes in the '34 World Series against the Detroit Tigers. In that dramatic 7-game set St. Louis whipped the hard-hitting Tigers 4 games to 3, with the Deans gaining credit for all the Cards victories: Dizzy finished with a Series record of 2–1 and a 1.73 ERA, and Daffy topped that with a 2–0 mark and a 1.00 ERA.

Freak Injury in All-Star Game Dooms Dizzy Dean's Big League Career

Dizzy and Daffy had strong seasons again in 1935, winning 28 and 19 games, respectively, and though the Cardinals finished with an excellent 96–58 record, the Chicago Cubs edged them out for the pennant by a 4-game margin. Paul's arm went bad after the '35 season. Then Dizzy's career took a sharp nosedive as the result of an injury in the 1937 All-Star Game.

Staged at Griffith Stadium, Washington, D.C., the All-Star was preceded by elaborate pregame ceremonies which featured President Franklin D. Roosevelt being driven out onto the field in an open car. An array of Cabinet officers, members of Congress, foreign diplomats, and assorted dignitaries were also in the box seats. A large delegation of Boy Scouts, attending the first National Jamboree in Washington, assisted in the impressive flag-raising.

For the first two frames the game was a pitchers' battle as Lefty Gomez (New York Yankees) and Dizzy Dean, making his second consecutive start for the N.L. (Diz was the winning pitcher in the '36 game), completed shutout innings.

Dean retired the first two batters in the third, but then Joe DiMaggio banged out his first All-Star hit, a line single. Lou Gehrig was the next batter up. Dean ran the count to 3-and-2 and then shook off a call by catcher Gabby Hartnett. Gehrig in 1937 was still at the peak of his brilliant career, and was no man to fool with. But the cocky Dean foolishly challenged him by throwing to his strength. Unloading a fastball instead of a sharp breaker, Dean watched Gehrig blast it way over the rightfield fence, a wallop that measured some 450 feet.

Obviously miffed with himself, Dizzy next tried to fog one past Earl Averill (Cleveland Indians). Averill, the "Rock of Snohomish," was expecting this fast one and rifled it back to the box. The ball struck Dean on the left foot and bounded away. Dean chased it down and nipped Averill at first on a close play, but when he reached the clubhouse he discovered his big toe was broken.

That play proved to be the turning point in Dean's career. He began pitching again long before the injury was healed completely. In doing so he was forced to change his motion and that placed an unnatural strain on his right arm and shoulder. Bursitis developed and he lost his great speed.

Dizzy was traded to the Cubs in 1938 and helped them win a pennant with a 7–1 record as a spot pitcher, but he had to depend on his new "dipsey doodle" pitch and sheer cunning. After that he hung on for a while, but by the time he was 30 his big league days were over—he was retired because of his lame arm. He struggled but he never came close to regaining the fastball which had terrified batters.

Jim "Doc" Ewell, who had spent more than 35 years as a big league trainer before retiring in 1979, talked about the strange case of Dizzy Dean in depth recently:

"Dean, unfortunately, took the old hard-nosed attitude and made the cardinal error of getting back into action long before he was physically ready. We really can't blame Dizzy for that catastrophic mistake. It just wasn't the fashion in those days to sit out too many games with an injury. . . . the idea was to grab a bat or a glove and run out onto the field, no matter what.

"Don't forget that Dean was only 26 at the time of that freak accident, and you'd assume that the club management also had a responsibility to keep a close eye on him during the recovery process. However, I doubt we'll see Dizzy Dean-type cases today because we've added a lot of sophistication to our training techniques.

"Nowadays if a star pitcher like Roger Clemens comes up with the slightest twinge in his arm or shoulder, trainers rush over to him like a rescue squad, and the managers and coaches won't let him pitch until he's 100 percent right. Pitchers in convalescence today can't even pick up a ball without getting permission. They always have a coach tailing them. If a pitching coach had really looked closely at Dean trying to throw after that All-Star Game, he would have known something was radically wrong.

"When I was the chief trainer with the Houston Astros, we never let a superstar like Cesar Cedeno, or any other player, get into a game unless he was physically right. Why should a ballclub take needless chances with multimillion-dollar ballplayers? It's crazy to play hurt and ruin a career.

"Sure, Dizzy Dean won 150 games in the majors, but if he had been made to wait a while longer after getting hit by that batted ball, maybe he could have won 300. To be brutally frank, big league baseball 50 years ago was in many ways run in a primitive style as compared with modern standards."

Dean's final big league stats came to 150 wins, 83 losses for a winning percentage of .644 and an ERA of 3.03, good enough to gain him Hall of Fame election in 1953. Interestingly, Paul won 50 games in his career (to go with 34 losses), so the two brothers managed to win exactly 200 games between them, though they were cut down by those terrible arm problems when they were still flowering as super-pitchers. Dizzy's total of 150 victories is the fewest of any Hall of Famer. Paul, like Dizzy, tried several comebacks and failed each time.

About the time that Dizzy Dean was being enshrined in the Hall of Fame, Hollywood tried to capture him on film in a movie titled "The Pride of St. Louis," with actor Dan Dailey starring in the role as "Ol' Diz." Bosley Crowther wrote in his review in *The New York Times*:

"The magnetic thing is the nature of a great, big lovable lug who plays baseball for a living and lives just to play—or talk—baseball. It is not Dizzy Dean the Cardinal pitcher, the powerhouse of the old Gashouse Gang, the man who won so many games in so many seasons, that is the hero of this film. It is Dizzy Dean the character, the whiz from the Ozark hills, the braggart, the woeful grammarian, the humble human being."

Dizzy Dean, Baseball Broadcaster, Mangler of the King's English

Once Dizzy Dean finally realized he was through as a pitcher early in the 1941 season (he pitched one inning for the Cubs in a game in mid-May and was tagged for 3 hits and 3 runs), he contemplated his future, and decided he wanted to become a baseball broadcaster.

The Falstaff Brewing Company, sponsors of the St. Louis Cardinals radio broadcasts, liked the idea of Dean's coming back to the Mound City, where he still ranked as a monumental heroic figure, and signed him to a contract to do play-by-play.

In his first appearance before a microphone early in June, Dean announced to his listeners, "I hope I'm as good a sports announcer as I was a pitcher," and then went on to charm his listeners with his peculiar brand of English. Runners "slud" into bases, pitchers "throwed" the ball, batters "swang," a hitter could look "mighty hitterish," or "stand confidentially" at the plate. Faking a double steal, two players "are now returning to their respectable bases."

Once he said "slid" correctly by mistake and he immediately "corrected" himself.

Radio listeners loved Dizzy's announcing, and the more he mangled the King's English the better they liked it. In 1942 Dean was judged by radio critics as "baseball's announcer with the worst diction," and in 1944, when he was doing both the Browns and Cardinals games, *The Sporting News* named Diz as "Announcer of the Year," and without any qualifiers.

He certainly didn't win any awards for objectivity, however, as he favored the Cards in particular. One day he roared into the microphone, "Well, here's Enos Slaughter, my ol' pal, walkin' up to the plate. . . . Come on now, Enos, knock the ball down this guy's throat!"

Dean committed his worst verbal atrocities in mispronouncing players' names: Stan Musial was "Moo-zell," Chico Carrasquel "that hitter with the three K's in his name." Tony Giuliani was rechristened "Julie-Annie," but Dean was at his most outrageous when he wrestled with himself trying to pronounce the name of Cubs pitcher Ed Hanyzewski. "I like to have broken my jaw tryin' to pronounce that one," he said, with a trace of desperation in his voice, "but I said his name by just holdin' my nose and sneezin'."

Diz, who hated paper work of any kind, never kept a scorecard or the batting "averuges." In this regard, he said: "I hate statics (statistics) . . . what I got to know I keep in my haid."

Dean's verbal miscues kept piling up with regularity, and as Curt Smith, a baseball broadcasting historian, said recently: "Each game with Dizzy Dean at the microphone assumed the air of a fresh performance, its set of realities choreographed by the Ozark encyclopedist."

According to Diz, this batter had an "unorsodock stance," give that shortstop "a sist," a play made adroitly was "non-challoted," and a one-handed catch was "a la carte." When Cleveland loaded the bases, "That loads the Injuns full o' bases," and "a manager argyin' with an umparr is like argyin' with a stump. . . . maybe you city folks don't know what a stump is. Wal, it's somethin' a tree has been cut down off of."

When the pace of a game slowed down, he often broke out into song, with his favorite number being "The Wabash Cannon Ball." He sang a bit off-key, by the way.

While Dean continued to be a big favorite among baseball fans throughout Missouri and points beyond, he did have his critics, and sharp ones at that. When the baseball commissioner, Kenesaw Mountain Landis, removed him from the network radio team for the all-St. Louis 1944 World Series, dubbing his diction "unfit for a national broadcaster," Diz, his feelings hurt, replied: "How can that commissar say I ain't eligible to broadcast? I ain't never met anybody that didn't know what ain't means."

In the summer of 1946, the English Teachers Association of Missouri termed Diz "a cultural illiterate" and demanded his removal from the air. In a formal complaint filed with the Federal Communications Commission, the schoolteachers stated that Dean's broadcasts were "replete with errors in grammar and syntax" and were having "a bad effect on the pupils."

But in the spirited public debate that followed, powerful voices were raised to champion Dizzy Dean, including the *St. Louis Globe Democrat,* whose editorials attacked the teachers' "smugness."

Norman Cousins, editor of the prestigious *Saturday Review of Literature,* also rushed to Dean's defense as he extended his personal approval to Diz' linguistic style. Cousins emphasized that Dean was an individualist, both as a ballplayer and as a broadcaster, called him "an American original," and advised the critics not to tamper with the great man's unique style that had gained such wide popularity.

Dean was allowed to keep his job, but he did promise to clean up his act, at least just a little bit. In a touching statement when the case was being closed, Diz said: "I see where some of those teachers is sayin' I'm butcherin' up the language a little. Just remember . . . when me and Paul was pickin' cotton in Arkansas, we didn't have no chance to go to school much. All I've got to say is that I'm real happy them kids is gettin' a chance today."

Dizzy Dean went on despite the criticism to enjoy a long and extremely successful career in baseball broadcasting, a career that stretched on for some 30-odd years in all, almost until the time of his death on July 17, 1973. He was invited to come to New York in 1950 to team up with Mel Allen in doing Yankee games. Then, beginning in 1955, he did the CBS Television "Game of the Week" for many seasons, and over a period of years worked on radio and television for other networks as well.

Commissioner Landis said earlier, as we pointed out, that Dean was not fit for national broadcasting, but an array of network executives thought otherwise.

Mel Allen recently recalled the antics of his old broadcasting partner: "Diz could get serious when *you* were talking, but once *he* took off solo, doing what passed for play-by-play, it was show biz time. Missing a pitch or two—that never fazed him. And he was smart, intelligent, and you never knew when he'd break out into song.

"Dean had a method and style all his own. Nothing like it before. . . . Just look around. Nothing like it since. That's because you couldn't get away with the stuff he did then . . . they'd throw you out of the booth with the mike strangled around your neck."

Mel Allen, sports broadcasting veteran of more than 50 years experience, also indicated that many of Dean's mistakes in English were probably preplanned: "Diz always knew what he was doing. The things he came up with—a guy 'sludding' into third—they were professional. He *knew* sliding was the correct form, but he *wanted* to goof up—it was a part of the vaudeville. But at the same time even more of his mistakes I'm sure were natural—the guy just didn't have much of an education. And he had an excitement about him."

This writer remembers when Dizzy Dean was doing the "Game of the Week" for CBS Television in the mid-1960s with Pee Wee Reese as his partner in the booth. By this time, Dean, never at a loss for words, had been behind the microphone for a quarter of a century and his style was definitely on the more polished side . . . not so many "sluds," "swangs" and "throweds" coming through at this point, but the grammar was still shaky and the speech colorful.

Asked one time if he was *the* greatest pitcher in baseball history, he replied: "Well, I don't know about that but I was right up there amongst 'um."

And among all the colorful and picturesque characters that came out of American baseball Jay Hanna "Dizzy" Dean was right up there with the likes of Casey Stengel and Babe Ruth.

The Sparrow in Casey's Cap

Charles Dillon "Casey" Stengel early in his career became renowned as one of baseball's true funny men—and one never knew when or where Stengel's ribald and irreverent sense of humor was going to break through.

After three years playing in the minors, Casey broke into the majors with the Brooklyn Dodgers at the tail end of the 1912 season. In his first game with the Dodgers, on September 17 against the Pittsburgh Pirates, Stengel enjoyed a banner day as he collected 4 singles and walked in 5 trips to the plate.

From that point on, Stengel became a Dodgers regular, and in 1916 he played a key role in helping Brooklyn to capture a pennant. Along the way he solidified his reputation as a prankster. Stengel became the bane of umpires and managers alike, with one of his favorite targets being Wilbert Robinson, the roly-poly pilot of the Dodgers.

One of Casey's pranks occurred at Daytona Beach, Florida, during spring training in 1915. On that occasion, Stengel was inspired by the recent feat of Washington catcher Gabby Street, who had caught a baseball dropped more than 500 feet from the top of the Washington Monument. The question now became: "Could a man catch a baseball dropped from an airplane?"

The airplane was supplied by Ruth Law, a noted pioneer woman flier, and the baseball was supplied by C. D. Stengel, except that it curiously became a grapefruit by the time it was dropped.

Stengel recalled: "Uncle Robbie was warming up this pitcher on the sidelines—we didn't have six coaches in those days. And this aviatrix—I believe it was the first one ever—flew over and dropped it. And Uncle Robbie saw it coming and waved everybody away like an outfielder and hollered, 'I've got it! I've got it!'

"Robbie got under this grapefruit, thinking it was a baseball, which hit him right on the pitcher's glove he put on, and the insides of it flew all over, seeds on his face and uniform, and flipped *him* right over on his back. Everybody came running up and commenced laughing, all except Robbie."

Before the beginning of the 1918 season, Stengel was traded to Pittsburgh and when Casey returned to Ebbets Field for the first time in an enemy uniform he was greeted by a rousing round of catcalls from the fans—and this inspired Casey to pull off one of his most fabled escapades.

When he was scheduled to bat for the first time, he *marched* up to home plate, bowed with exaggerated courtliness to the grandstand, doffed his cap—and out flew a sparrow. Casey had given them the bird!

On another occasion, as legend has it, he went out to right-field at Ebbets Field, spotted a drainage hole and suddenly disappeared from sight. A few moments later he rose majestically, a manhole cover under his arm, just in time to catch a fly ball!

Later, when he became a hard-boiled manager, Stengel looked back on his wayward years as a rambunctious player and said:

"Now that I am a manager, I see the error of my youthful ways. If any player pulled that stuff on me now, I would probably fine his ears off."

Casey often spoke in a non-stop style that came to be known as "Stengelese"—a kind of convoluted doubletalk laced with ambiguous antecedents, a lack of proper names (he generally referred to a player as "that guy"), and a liberal use of adjectives like "amazing" and "terrific."

He drew on baseball lore dating back to pre-World War I days, and would clinch points in rhetoric by declaring with finality: "You could look it up." And when a listener's attention waned, he would immediately recapture it by exclaiming, "Now, let me ask you," and would be off and running again.

Warren Spahn, who pitched for Casey Stengel at the beginning and end of his illustrious career (with the Boston Braves in 1942 and with the New York Mets in 1965) told this writer recently:

"Casey Stengel may have been a funny man in the eyes of the fans and sportswriters, but when you played for him you saw the real Casey. He was a tough and demanding manager. When he lectured us in the clubhouse or on the field there was nothing funny about him . . . he was all business. That's why he was a great manager. He had an amazingly deep knowledge of the game, and his humor off the field was a kind of self-effacing cover."

Rookie Mantle Insults Casey

When Mickey Mantle came up with the New York Yankees at the beginning of the 1951 season, he was one of the most highly touted rookie ballplayers of the 20th century.

Only 19, Mickey already had two years experience in professional ranks and had enjoyed a banner season in 1950 with Joplin, Missouri, of the Class C Western Association, hitting a league-leading .383 and knocking in 136 runs.

Mantle, a murderous switch-hitter labeled "can't miss," began the '51 campaign for the Yanks in good style at bat as he delivered key base hits and drove in his share of runs. Manager Casey Stengel, however, noted that Mantle's work at his rightfield position left something to be desired, so Stengel spent many hours personally coaching Mickey on the finer points of patrolling the outer pastures.

One day in early June, Casey was showing Mickey how to field balls that caromed off the rightfield barrier at Yankee Stadium. Stengel, wearing an outfielder's glove, set himself into playing position and said, "This is the way I used to play bounces that ricocheted off this barrier."

Mantle looked down at Casey, not believing that this wizened old man could have ever been a ballplayer and blurted: "Like hell you did!" Casey was silent. (Actually Stengel had played rightfield in the new Yankee Stadium in the 1923 World Series with the New York Giants when they clashed with the Yankees.)

The very next day Casey sent Mickey down to the minors where he spent the next six weeks with the Kansas City Blues of the American Association before Stengel called him back up to New York.

Stengel said later of the incident, "When I show a player how to do something and he gets smart-alecky with me, back down to the bushes he goes . . . and I don't care who he is."

Mickey learned his lesson the hard way and from that point on he made it a point to listen with respect to his manager.

During the late 1950s when Mickey Mantle was at the peak of his career as a power-hitting Yankees outfielder, he made sports headlines when he signed his first contract calling for a six-figure amount, exactly $100,000. Just a generation ago, six-figure salaries for a full season's play were reserved for the really big diamond stars like Mantle, Joe DiMaggio, Stan Musial and Ted Williams. Today, that kind of money won't even cover the salary of a third-string catcher.

In fact, each member of the 1988 Los Angeles Dodgers received nearly $109,000 as a winning share of the 5-game World Series. And each member of the Oakland A's, who bowed to the Dodgers in the '88 Series, received a share amounting to just over $86,000.

Mike Sciosca, the Dodgers catcher, who averaged .257 in 1988 while poking out only 3 homers and driving in 35 runs, signed a contract calling for a cool $1 million in 1989. That's inflation for you!

Cobb's Day

During a Detroit Tigers "Old-Timers Day" staged at Briggs Stadium in July 1951, a young reporter went up to Ty Cobb (a lifetime .367 hitter and charter Hall of Fame member) and asked: "Mr. Cobb, what do you think you would hit if you were playing today?"

"Oh, about .300," answered Cobb.

"Is that all?" said the reporter incredulously.

Cobb countered without batting an eye: "Well, don't forget I'm 65 years old."

Riding on a Train with the Babe Can Be Dangerous

Babe Ruth liked to live life to the fullest and often his appetite for pleasure and frolic proved to be his undoing. He became the world's best known athlete not only for his prodigious home-run hitting, but also because of his outrageous antics on and off the field. The public's appetite for any bit of news about "The Sultan of Swat" was insatiable.

On one occasion, for example, after a night on the town in Manhattan, he hailed a cab and after he was deposited at his apartment door, the Babe reached into his pocket and handed the cabbie what he thought was a $10 bill.

"Keep the change!" boomed the generous Babe . . . the cab fare had come to only about $2.

The taxi driver's eyes almost popped out of his head as he glanced at the bill. With a lightning-quick motion he grabbed it and raced off with his hack.

Unfortunately, because his eyes were a bit glazed over, Ruth didn't realize until later that he had given the driver a $1,000 bill!

"I'd better look at my money a little more carefully before I spend it," the Babe said with a touch of remorse in his voice.

As the 1925 season dawned, George Herman Ruth, then 30, was at the height of his career. In his ten major league seasons he had succeeded in becoming *the* dominant force in the game.

In a game at Tampa toward the end of spring training, the Babe had slammed a couple of tape-measure homers. He then went on to celebrate by gorging himself on a yard or two of hot dogs and what amounted to nearly a bucket of soda pop.

This time the Bambino really overdid it. He became violently ill and was rushed to a New York hospital for an emergency stomach operation. Front page headlines everywhere recorded Ruth's illness as a national crisis, with clergymen of all faiths holding special services calling for Ruth's recovery. The Babe came close to death, but as one of the surgeons on the case said, "Only his youth and strength saved him." This was known as "The Bellyache Heard Round The World."

Ruth didn't get into the Yankees lineup until early June,

missing the first six weeks of the season. And for the first two or three weeks, he had trouble keeping his average over .250, because he was still weak from the effects of the stomach operation.

The Babe's disposition suffered and this led to memorable clashes with Yankee manager Miller Huggins. Among other things, the two had a number of dugout shouting matches, but little "Hug," a veteran of 25 years in the majors as a player and manager (he stood 5 feet 4 inches and weighed 145 pounds soaking wet), backed down to no man, not even to the great Babe Ruth.

Matters came to a head toward mid-August on a long train trip home from St. Louis (where the Yanks had played the Browns) when Ruth tried to throw Huggins off the moving train. The Babe perpetrated this outrage half-jokingly, but Hug was not amused and slapped G.H.R. with a $5,000 fine, the most costly ever levied on a ballplayer to that date.

Ruth was absolutely livid and blustered into the office of Yankee owner Colonel Jacob Ruppert, threatening to quit if the fine wasn't rescinded, and Huggins fired. "The fine sticks and Huggins stays," Ruppert told him in no uncertain terms.

The Babe knew when he was licked, and from that point he acted like an All-American Boy Scout and finished the season with 25 homers and a .290 average, not bad at all considering his horrendous start.

Nevertheless, Ruth's absence from so many games hurt the Yankees as they finished a dismal 7th in 1925, posting a losing 69–85 (.448) record.

The Bambino went all out in 1926 to redeem himself, enjoying a banner year as he paced the Bronx Bombers to a pennant, batting a robust .372 and leading the league with 47 homers and 145 RBIs. (Interestingly, the Yankees then proceeded to pile up 39 consecutive winning seasons, a record string for any team in professional sports. It wasn't until 1965 that New York dropped below the .500 mark again.)

The Yankees clashed with the St. Louis Cardinals in the 1926 World Series, and after Huggins' charges whipped the Cards 2 games out of 3 in St. Louis to take an overall 3–2 lead, the New Yorkers were in a jovial mood on the 1,000-mile train ride back to the Big City. Ruth was in particularly high spirits and, after having had several high-powered drinks along the way, he spotted Colonel Jake Ruppert by himself in the club car. Ruth went over and gave the Colonel a bear hug. By the time he was through mauling the Yankees' distinguished-looking owner he had succeeded in ripping the Colonel's tailored shirt off his back.

Ruth and his teammates had a good laugh over this incident, but Ruppert was absolutely furious. Unfortunately, the Yankees dropped the next 2 games to the Cardinals and lost the World Series 4–3. Again, Jake Ruppert was not amused.

There is one Babe Ruth train ride, however, that has not been as widely publicized as the Huggins and Ruppert incidents. This particular rail journey occurred in about 1930 during one of the post-season barnstorming trips down South that Ruth himself had organized with other major leaguers.

One late afternoon as the train chugged through a small town, the Babe spotted a group of teen-aged boys playing a pick-up baseball game in an open field. Since the train had to stop for water, Ruth jumped out of the train, walked over to the field and got himself involved in the game.

In the process, he gave the boys tips on batting, fielding, throwing and sliding. Ruth took off his suit jacket and demonstrated the techniques of sliding into a base as he kicked up a minor sandstorm in the process.

After 35 to 40 minutes, with the train more than ready to proceed, the Babe dusted himself off and reluctantly got back into his car.

"Who was that man?" asked one of the boys.

"Why, that was Babe Ruth himself!" came the answer.

"I don't believe it," said another incredulously. He should have believed it, for this episode actually happened and was filmed by one of Ruth's teammates who had a movie camera with him. He recorded nearly the entire scene on film, a film that has been shown periodically on commercial television.

Stories about Babe Ruth showing kindness to kids are legion. The Babe was raised in an orphanage, experienced much unhappiness as a boy, and as an adult compensated for this barren spot in his early life by going out of his way to treat youngsters with a great deal of fatherly affection.

Babe Ruth achieved the rare combination of hitting for

power and average. His best season for average came in 1923 when he finished at .393 while drilling 41 homers and driving in 131 runs. Over his 22-year career (1914–35), the Bambino averaged a healthy .342, a percentage good enough to give him ninth place on the all-time list of batters who came to the plate officially at least 5,000 times.

Once, when discussing hitting with a reporter, the Bambino declared: "Hell, I coulda averaged .600, but all my hits would have been singles."

Babe Ruth established so many records that it requires several pages just to list them all, but one of his least known records concerns his hitting accomplishments while he was a pitcher. The Babe is the only pitcher in big league history (with at least 100 games on the mound to his credit) to have hit .300 or better lifetime. In 163 games as a pitcher (mostly with the Boston Red Sox from 1914 through 1919), Ruth averaged .304. His batting prowess is what led to his sale to the Yankees in 1920.

Wes Ferrell, generally conceded to be the best hitting pitcher on a career basis, could manage only .280 average. In a 15-year career (1927–41), Ferrell also set a pair of home run records for a pitcher: most in one season, 9 in 1931, and most in a career, 38.

Al Simmons' "Foot-in-the-Bucket" Stance

"He'll never be a hitter," chided the critics in 1924 as they watched Al Simmons, rookie Philadelphia Athletics outfielder, take batting practice in spring training.

The 22-year-old Simmons had averaged better than .360 in three minor league seasons, but his unorthodox batting style bothered his managers and coaches.

Simmons, batting righthanded, is said to have kept one "foot-in-the-bucket" (an affliction common to sandlotters)—that is, he kept his forward foot (left foot) at a pronounced angle toward third base rather than forward, toward the pitcher. This stance, however, enabled Simmons to keep his front foot free so that he could hit to any field.

Simmons went on to hit .308 in his rookie year with the A's, and in his second season he collected 253 base hits (the most ever by a righthanded hitter) and averaged .384. When A's manager Connie Mack was asked what he thought of Simmons' "foot-in-the-bucket" stance, he replied: "I don't care if he stands on his head so long as he keeps murdering that ball!"

Simmons never changed his batting style through a 20-year career in which he banged out 2,927 hits, averaged .334 and drove in 1,827 runs. He won back-to-back batting titles in 1930–31 when he averaged .381 and .390, respectively, as he paced the A's to American League pennants in both years.

Though Al Simmons may have looked like a rank sandlotter at the plate he was dreaded by every pitcher in the league. He gained election to baseball's Hall of Fame in 1953.

Hank Ruszkowski, a big righthanded-hitting catcher who had several trials with the Cleveland Indians from 1944 to 1947, had an even more peculiar batting stance than the one used by Al Simmons. Ruszkowski used to hold his bat with the barrel touching the ground as he waited for the pitch. While watching him in that stance in an exhibition game at Cleveland Stadium, we saw him hit a home run that carried at least 425 feet.

Batting stances can be a relative matter.

A gala parade through downtown Sacramento helped kick off the start of the 1903 Pacific Coast League season.

(Rare photo from the collection of Douglas M. McWilliams, Berkeley, California)

Inaugural Game in Pacific Coast League, 1903

Leaving the State House Hotel for the ballpark are the Sacramento Sacts and the Oakland Oaks after special ceremonies marking the opening day of Pacific Coast League play in Sacramento. The Oaks won the game, 7–4.

In that inaugural 1903 season, the Los Angeles Angels won the pennant by posting a staggering 133–78 record to finish 27½ games ahead of second-place Sacramento, who came in at 105–105. Every other entrant in the six-team PCL finished below .500, with Oakland bringing up the rear at 89–126. The final games of the marathon season were played on November 29th! After nearly 90 consecutive seasons of play, the Pacific Coast League is still going strong, but in recent years the schedules have been cut to a more modest 144 games.

○ **6** ○
PITCHERS KNOW IT ALL

Lefty Grove's Temper Is as Famous as His Pitching Prowess

Robert Moses ("Lefty") Grove was as well known for his hot temper as for his brilliant pitching in a major league career that spanned 17 seasons (1925–41). Lefty won exactly 300 games and lost only 141, good for a lofty winning percentage of .680. Moreover, he fashioned a lifetime ERA of 3.06 in an era when hitters dominated the game. He led the American League for the lowest ERA in a record 9 seasons.

Grove spent the first nine years of his big league career with the Philadelphia Athletics and the remaining eight with the Boston Red Sox.

Born in a small town in the Appalachian Mountain country of Western Maryland, Grove developed a suspicious nature and a mean disposition. While with the Athletics, he gave Connie Mack, one of the gentlest of all managers, the absolute fits.

Grove, as the ace of the Athletics pitching staff, felt privileged to be the only player on the team to call the venerable manager "Connie." To all others, it had to be "Mr. Mack."

When trying for his 17th consecutive victory in 1931, which would have been a new American League record, Grove lost the game by a 1-0 count to St. Louis when leftfielder Jim Moore misjudged a fly ball, allowing the lone run to score.

After the defeat, Grove charged into the clubhouse like a mad bull. He slammed doors, kicked the water pail, threw his spikes into the locker and roared. When his catcher Mickey Cochrane said, "Hard luck, Lefty," he unleashed a torrent of profanity that sent Mickey retreating and mumbling to himself.

When Connie Mack entered the clubhouse, the manager employed some of the strongest language he ever used in trying to quiet down the volcanic Grove when he said, "Shut up, Robert!"

When that had no effect, Mack took the problem in hand further. He tried to solve the situation, not by pitying Grove, but by praising Browns righthander Dick Coffman, who had allowed the A's only 3 hits. "Robert, didn't Coffman pitch a wonderful game today? We only got 3 singles and we wouldn't have scored a run if we had still been playing."

Grove, now struggling to control his anger, agreed at least that Coffman deserved to win. That calmed him down.

When Lefty Grove joined the Red Sox, he was approaching his mid-thirties, but his disposition was just as nasty as ever. He certainly wasn't mellowing with age. One time in a 1935 game at Detroit, shortstop-manager Joe Cronin tried to stop a hot smash off the bat of Hank Greenberg by getting down on one knee so that he could at least trap the ball. The ball struck Cronin on the knee cap and ricocheted off into left-centerfield.

"Okay, Cronin, get up off your knees and field your position like a man!" he screamed from the pitcher's mound. Grove could have waited to get into the dugout or clubhouse to chastise Cronin for the misplay which allowed 2 runs to score and cost Grove the game.

In Cronin's defense, it should be pointed out that the vogue in those days was for infielders to get down on one knee—or on both knees—to field sizzling ground balls. You won't see infielding of that type very often today.

Herman Wehmeier's brushback pitches failed to intimidate rookie Eddie Mathews.

(Courtesy Everitt J. Helm)

Rookie Refuses To Be Intimidated by Pitcher

"Who's the *gutsiest* player you've ever seen perform on a baseball diamond?" asked a grizzled scout during an informal discussion among veteran baseball men at Oakland's Alameda County Stadium before the start of the 1987 All-Star Game.

Another senior scout with decades of experience to his credit got up and answered without a second's hesitation, "That player, in my estimation, has got to be Eddie Mathews." He then went on to give specifics along these lines.

Mathews, a lefthanded power-hitting third baseman came up to the Boston Braves as a 20-year-old rookie in 1952, and National League pitchers went all out immediately to test his mettle. In one of his first big league games, Mathews faced big righthanded fastball hurler Herman Wehmeier of the Cincinnati Reds at Crosley Field. Wehmeier had a reputation for wildness, having already led the league in walks twice, and in '52 he was on his way to leading the circuit in that department again. He also had the reputation of being a "head-hunter."

Wehmeier's first pitch was a blazing high inside fastball that went straight at Mathews' head, but Eddie instinctively dropped to the ground in a heap to avoid being decapitated. He dusted himself off, and got right back into the batter's box. Wehmeier's second pitch speeded in at the same spot and again Mathews fell to the ground. After he dusted himself off, he clenched his teeth in fierce determination, dug himself a firm toehold at the plate and waited for another delivery. This time the pitch came straight down the middle; Eddie caught hold of it squarely and whacked a vicious line drive that went far over the rightfield wall for a homer—the first of his career.

From that moment on, National League moundsmen grew to respect Eddie Mathews. In all, Mathews slammed out 512 homers in his 17 years in the majors, and one of the biggest had to be that shot off Herm Wehmeier at the very dawn of his career. It didn't surprise anyone that he was eventually elected to the Hall of Fame at Cooperstown.

Hubbell's Screwball "Shortens" His Career

Young Carl Hubbell threw lefthanded and batted right, pitched and played the outfield for the Meeker (Oklahoma) high school team when he wasn't busy with farm chores. It wasn't until he was all of 20 when he launched his pro career.

With Oklahoma City in 1925, Hubbell appeared in 45 games, pitched 284 innings and finished at 17–13. The Detroit Tigers, thinking Hubbell showed some promise for all his frail appearance, bought his contract and invited him to spring training in 1926.

Ty Cobb, then managing Detroit, was not overly impressed with Carl's work, and had him shipped off to Toronto of the Class AA International League where he compiled a mediocre 7–7 record. Hubbell appeared at spring training with the Tigers again in 1927 and the new manager, George Moriarty, was impressed even less and sent Carl down to Decatur, Illinois, of the Class B Three-Eye League. At Decatur he fashioned an excellent 14-7 record with a very low 2.53 ERA.

It was along about here that Hubbell, now 24, realizing he was going nowhere, began tinkering with the screwball. John Drebinger, who covered Hubbell's entire career for *The New York Times,* said: "It intrigued Carl's studious nature to see batters become hopelessly confused by a pitch that curved one way when they expected it to go the other."

When Tiger manager Moriarty inspected Hub's screwball again in spring training 1928, he declared: "Young man, if you persist in throwing that pitch, your days in baseball are numbered. It is certain to ruin your arm."

And with that the Tigers sold Hubbell outright to Beaumont of the Texas League, without having used him in a single championship game in a Detroit uniform.

Relying on his newly refined screwball, Hubbell blossomed at Beaumont as he went 12–9 by mid-season with a 2.97 ERA. He managed to control his pet pitch almost perfectly as he walked only 45 and struck out 116 in 185 innings of work.

The New York Giants, desperately in need of pitching to stay in the National League pennant race, took note of these happenings, and bought Hubbell's contract from Beaumont in

In throwing his baffling "screwball," "King" Carl Hubbell placed so much pressure on his elbow that he eventually bent his left arm completely out of shape.

mid-July for $40,000, a big chunk of cash in those days. Under Giant manager John McGraw's direction, Hub finished the '28 season with a strong 10–6 (ERA 2.83) mark.

The Giants closed out the season in second place, just 2 games behind pennant-winning St. Louis, with Manager McGraw observing: "If Carl Hubbell had started out the year with us, we would have finished first easily."

Curiously enough, George Moriarty's prediction that the screwball would ruin Hubbell's arm proved to be correct. Throwing a pitch like that places enormous stress on the arm, especially on and around the elbow region. When Hub retired after the 1943 season, his left arm was grotesquely bent out of shape; it looked like a scythe hanging down from his side. "I would have liked to pitch a while longer, but it was tough throwing a ball with a crooked arm," he said later.

However, in those 16 seasons with the Giants he had established himself as one of the greatest lefthanders in baseball history. Hubbell won 253, lost 154 for a winning percentage of .622, and he fashioned a skinny 2.98 ERA in this heavy-hitting era. In three World Series (1933, 1936–37), "King Carl" went 4–2, compiling a 1.79 ERA in 50 innings of work.

He set a modern major league record when he won 24 straight games: 16 for the last half of the '36 season and 8 more at the start of the '37 campaign. He won more than 20 games in 5 successive seasons (1933–37), reaching a high-water mark in 1936 with a glittering 26–6 posting.

Hubbell, known as "The Meal Ticket" because of his reliability, enjoyed his greatest moments of all, perhaps, in the 1934 All-Star Game at the Polo Grounds when he struck out five of the greatest sluggers in American League history *in succession*: Babe Ruth, Lou Gehrig, Jimmie Foxx, Al Simmons and Joe Cronin (all five are in baseball's Hall of Fame).

The unfortunate five were obviously mystified by Hub's screwball which they had not seen before.

Vernon "Lefty" Gomez, another great southpaw, explained how Hubbell's screwball worked in these terms: "Carl was a pitcher's pitcher . . . we all admired him because he had absolute powers of concentration while working, and he had persevered for years to master pinpoint control.

"Hub's type of screwball is a pitch thrown with a reverse

twist of the wrist which makes the ball break in a direction opposite to that of a normally thrown curveball. Since Carl was a southpaw, the pitch broke in toward a lefthanded batter instead of away from him—then against a righthanded hitter, the ball broke away from him instead of in to him. Hubbell was especially tough against righthanded swingers who would normally expect to murder a southpaw curveballer.

"No one had thrown the so-called 'fadeaway' pitch, or 'reverse curve,' so effectively since Christy Mathewson and he was a righthander.

"Carl ordinarily relied on his screwball in clutch situations only . . . if he threw it all the time, batters would have gotten used to it and belted the ball all over the lot. But the pitch was new to the American Leaguers in that 1934 All-Star Game, and old Hub got them all tied up in knots."

Lefty Gomez himself was quite a comic. His nemesis was the big Red Sox slugger Jimmie Foxx. Gomez said, "He has muscles in his hair." During one game with Bill Dickey catching, Gomez kept shaking off Dickey's signals. Finally, Bill ran out to the mound and said, "What do you want to throw?"

"I don't wanna throw nothin'," Gomez said. "Maybe he'll get tired of waiting and leave."

○ **7** ○

BASEBALL IS
EVERYWHERE

3.6 Million Fans in the Stands?

When the Chicago Cubs scheduled their first night game ever at Wrigley Field for Monday, August 8, 1988, they placed 8,000 tickets on public sale which could be ordered by phone only the day before the game. More than 1.8 million phone calls were made to the Cubs' ticket office on that fateful day, and Illinois Bell officials said that was a record for calls to the same number on one day.

The Cubs could have sold 3.6 million tickets for their first night game since each order had to be for two ducats. Unfortunately, Wrigley Field has a seating capacity of only 37,272.

George Will, Cub Fan

Did you know that George Will, the political TV commentator and syndicated columnist, is a rabid Chicago Cub fan? When we ran into him at the 1988 All-Star Game in Cincinnati, we talked.

Q. George, did you collect baseball cards as a boy?

A. Yes, and I wish I had them now.

Q. What happened to them?

A. My mother threw them out!

Q. How does baseball relate to politics?

A. I got tough by suffering with the Chicago Cubs for so many years.

All-Star Day in the Furnace in K.C.

Kansas City hosted its first-ever All-Star Game in 1960 (July 11), and the local fans were so anxious to see the big league stars that the 101-degree afternoon heat didn't stop them from turning out en masse. Municipal Stadium was packed to capacity with a paid attendance of nearly 31,000. And it was so hot that the TV cameras had to be wrapped in ice to prevent them from overheating.

The National League bats were as hot as the weather in the first inning as starter Bill Monbouquette (Boston Red Sox) was raked for 3 runs. Willie Mays' triple and Ernie Banks' homer were the key hits for the N.L. The Nationals got to Monbouquette for another run in the second when Del Crandall (Chicago Cubs) picked on a fastball and lined it over the left-field screen for a homer.

"When Monbouquette came back into the dugout after that second inning, we thought he was going to pass out from the heat—and he damn near did," recalled Jim Ewell, one of the American League trainers who was then with the K.C. Athletics. "We had to give him a strong whiff of oxygen and repeated splashes of ammonia water on the back of his neck to get him back to normal. The official temperature may have been 101, but it was even hotter on the playing surface," Ewell remembered.

Chuck Estrada (Baltimore Orioles) took over the A.L. pitching duties in the third and yielded another run . . . Ernie Banks' double was the key hit in this inning.

The A.L. came back with 3 runs in the late innings, but in the bottom of the 9th a Junior Circuit rally fizzled in the sizzling heat as reliever Vern Law (Pittsburgh) retired the side without any damage being done. The final score came to 5–3.

Trainer Jim Ewell also recalls: "I've never seen so many players bushed at the end of 9 innings. Despite the fact that the park was almost like a furnace, they all played hard, and we were lucky that no one suffered heatstroke. Willie Mays, who had 3 hits and did plenty of running on the bases and in the field, especially needed the trainers' attention at the end of the game—we gave him the oxygen and ammonia water treatment and he snapped right back to normal."

Even Hotter in St. Louis
for the 1966 All-Star Game

St. Louis was chosen as the locale for the 1966 All-Star Game for two reasons: to help commemorate the city's bicentennial and to celebrate the opening, earlier in the season, of the new Busch Memorial Stadium on the Mississippi Riverfront.

Most of the nearly 50,000 fans who attended the game remembered the searing 106-degree heat as well as they did the National League's 2–1 victory in a 10-inning pitchers' battle.

Just how hot was it in St. Louis during that scorching July 12 afternoon? Brooks Robinson recalled recently: "Busch Stadium was a hotbox that day. Early on, our batboy passed out cold in the dugout, and I saw fans in the stands pass out during the course of the game." The broiling heat was so high that over 150 persons required first aid at the stadium.

Jim Ewell, then the Houston Astros' chief trainer, who served the National League that memorable day, says: "It was sure hotter 'n hell in St. Louis for that game. We had our cold packs, smelling salts, and oxygen ready for players who began to feel woozy. I remember working on Hank Aaron and Willie Mays more than a little toward the middle of the game. Those two guys hung in there for the whole 10 innings. Remember what I said about that 1960 game in Kansas City, when it was also over 100 degrees. The true stars give it all they've got, no matter what the weather is."

August A. Busch, Jr., owner of the St. Louis Cardinals and president of the Anheuser-Busch Brewery, wasn't all that unhappy about the extreme heat on that sultry midsummer day, however. "We sold a record amount of beer that afternoon . . . the fans couldn't get enough of it," he chortled.

George Bush, Good Glove, Weak Bat at Yale

George Herbert Walker Bush, the 41st President of the United States, has the distinction of being the nation's only chief executive to have won his letter in baseball in college. Bush, a lefthanded thrower, righthanded hitter (an odd combination), scintillated as a first baseman for the Yale University varsity nine in 1947–48 and had the additional distinction of being chosen as the team's captain in '48.

Bush, in fact, comes from a long line of athletes. For starters, his father, the late Prescott Bush, who represented Connecticut in the U.S. Senate from 1952 to 1963, batted clean-up for the Yale team in 1917, while four of George Bush's maternal uncles also played baseball for Yale. The President's mother, Dorothy Walker Bush, a sprightly 89 in 1989, was a ferocious softball player. The day her first son, Prescott, was born, she hit a home run in a tightly contested game at Kennebunkport, Maine, and after she circled the bases she announced it was time to go to the hospital. "Pressy" came in at a healthy ten pounds later that day.

With father Prescott and mother Dorothy leading the way, their entire brood, consisting of four sons and a daughter, became involved in nearly the entire spectrum of athletics. According to daughter Nancy Ellis, in the Bush family athletic education begins "at birth." Intrafamily competitions have included not only the obvious ones—softball, touch football, tennis and table tennis—but also tiddly-winks, fishing tournaments, indoor golf putting (with plastic cups set about the house), horseshoe pitching and knee football (played, as the name implies, on one's knees). A prime knee-football player was Bucky, the youngest Bush brother, who at Hotchkiss prep school weighed more than 250 pounds. Standing lamps were forever being toppled. It's a wonder, recalled George Bush, that the family's houses in Kennebunkport and Greenwich, Connecticut, stood up under all the heavy punishment.

The future president spent four years at Phillips Academy at Andover, Massachusetts, where he captained the basketball and soccer teams, played varsity baseball and served as president of the senior class.

When he graduated from Andover in June 1942, Bush chose not to accept immediate admission to Yale, but rather enlisted in the U.S. Navy, and after completing flight training he served as a bomber pilot in the Pacific Theatre for nearly two years. Toward the end of World War II, Bush became a Navy flight instructor at Norfolk, Virginia, and then entered Yale in the fall of 1945.

Somehow, young Bush passed up baseball in favor of soccer as a freshman, but then concentrated on baseball for the next two years. (On an accelerated program, he graduated in three years.)

Lots of competition existed among excellent athletes in the post-World War II era and topnotch baseball teams represented Yale. The team was coached by Ethan Allen, a former major league outfielder, who had averaged an even .300 in his 13-year playing career (1926–38).

Bush, who attended many a major baseball event as Vice President (including Opening Day Games, All-Star Games, the Playoff Series of both leagues and the World Series) recalled his Yale baseball days at a press conference staged before the August 9, 1981 All-Star Game played at Cleveland: "I made the team primarily because of my fielding ability . . . as a hitter I was a bit on the mediocre side."

One of his proudest possessions today is his George McQuinn first-baseman's mitt from Yale, oiled and ready for use, stashed in his desk in the Oval Office.

Yale was a true baseball power during Bush's tenure there as the Elis won the NCAA Eastern Division Championship in '47 and '48 with regular season records of 17-8-1 and 17-7-1, respectively. Those two NCAA Eastern titles gained Yale berths in the first two College World Series over played, which were contested at Kalamazoo, Michigan.

In '47 Yale was considered the underdog when it was matched with the University of California, and sure enough the Yaleys proceeded to lose both games (in the best of three series) by scores of 17–4 and 8–7. At the Cleveland All-Star press conference, Bush recalled the second game against California: "We walked the eighth hitter in the Cal lineup to get to Jackie Jensen who was pitching. He hit the ball so far that it must be still rolling out there somewhere in western

Capt. G.H.W. Bush '48

George Bush, 41st President of the United States, captained the Yale varsity baseball team in 1948 as he scintillated at first base, batting righthanded and throwing left, an odd combination.

Michigan. We blamed Coach Ethan Allen, of course, for making a bad call."

Jackie Jensen, then better known as an All-American full-back, went on to star in the big leagues for the New York Yankees, Washington Senators and Boston Red Sox. Interestingly, Jensen is the only athlete to have played in the College World Series, the Rose Bowl, the major league All-Star Game and the World Series.

For the 1947 season, Bush batted a less-than-robust .239 (21 for 88) with 1 homer, 16 runs scored and 9 RBIs, but he was considered a real Fancy Dan around first base.

Bush had perhaps his best day on the field in an April 4, 1948 game played against North Carolina State University at Raleigh when he singled, doubled and tripled and drove in 5 in a 9–6 Eli victory. He was flawless in the field with 11 putouts. Moreover, he stretched and jumped to save Yale infielders two or three errors on errant throws.

After that game, the major league scouts in attendance converged upon Bush to find out if the 23-year-old 6-foot-2-inch, 195-pound first baseman was interested in playing professional ball. Ethan Allen, now 84, recently recalled that historic day: "That confirmed my suspicions of how little scouts know about hitting. They thought they had uncovered a star until they checked his batting average. . . . George Bush was a line-drive hitter, but the trouble was that he didn't hit too many line drives . . . he always had problems trying to hit the curve ball, but at the same time he always worked harder than anybody else to improve."

In the '48 College World Series, Yale took on the University of Southern California, led by Rod Dedeaux, one of the most renowned coaches in college baseball history. USC's mascot and batboy was a bright-eyed 14-year-old youngster named George "Sparky" Anderson, who later gained fame as manager of the Cincinnati Reds and Detroit Tigers.

In a recent interview Dedeaux recalled that Game One of that best-of-three series had "one of the most exciting finales in College World Series history." The game was tied 1–1 at the end of 8 innings, but USC scored 2 runs in the top of the 9th to take a 3–1 lead. In the bottom of the 9th, Yale loaded the bases with nobody out when infielder Gerard Breen lined a shot back to the pitcher who started a triple play to abruptly end the game.

"Guess who was in the on-deck circle ready to hit next?" Dedeaux asked rhetorically. "Why, nobody other than George Herbert Walker Bush!"

Bush himself said of that incident when at the '81 All-Star Game press conference: "If I had gotten a chance to hit in that critical ninth inning situation and delivered—well, who knows, maybe I would have gone on to pro ball after all."

Yale won the second game by a decisive 8–3 count, but then lost the third game and the series to USC in a 9–2 rout.

During the '48 regular season, Bush had improved his hitting, averaging a respectable .264 (23 for 87) with 1 homer, 2 triples, 6 doubles, 15 runs scored and 14 RBIs, but his performance in the College World Series against USC left something to be desired as he "took the collar," going 0 for 12.

Yale University's athletic department is proud to list George Bush as one of its most famous lettermen, though at the same time it has tried to "cover-up" that sad little stat.

Over the years Bush has kept in touch with members of that '48 Yale team, with reunions having been held on a regular basis. In fact, all surviving members of that NCAA Eastern championship squad were invited to attend his Presidential inauguration on January 20, 1989. Sometimes he even calls them on the phone from "Air Force One" just to say "Hello."

Several members of that '48 team went on to play professional baseball, including outfielder Dick Tettelbach, who saw brief service with the New York Yankees and Washington Senators.

Several years ago, Bush as Vice President threw out the first ball in the New York Mets Opening Day game at Shea Stadium. The ball went wild, hit several feet in front of the plate and bounced past the catcher.

A while later Dick Tettelbach ran into Bush at a campaign rally and said: "That throw you made at Shea Stadium was terrible . . . and I always thought you had a good arm."

Bush replied with a smile: "I blame it all on that bulletproof vest I was wearing. The Secret Service made me put that damned thing on . . . and I consider that a legitimate excuse for making a bad throw."

Eight years ago, Warren Spahn and Bill Dickey needled Bush into playing in an Old-Timers game at Denver.

"When Tony Oliva came up," recalled Bush, "the second baseman kept yelling at me, 'Get back.' I said, 'Back? I'm on the damned grass. Whaddaya want?' But the second baseman said, 'Back. This guy can still hit.' And damned if Oliva didn't pull one right down the line."

Though Oliva was 44 then and Bush 57, the President's memory of the play is that he just wishes he had had his McQuinn Trapper. "My excuse on this part is I had a brand new mitt—knocked the ball down—should have had it clean."

Bush dove to his left, backhanded the smash, then flipped to Milt Pappas for the out on a play that brought the crowd to its feet. Since Bush already had a solid single to center in his only at-bat, he decided to walk right off the field and into a glorious and permanent retirement. Like his old fishing friend, Ted Williams, Bush knew when to quit.

The Russians Take Up Baseball

The Russians as a nation take great pride in their athletic skills and demonstrate their awesome athletic prowess at international tournaments regularly, especially during the quadrennial Summer Olympic Games.

Since baseball will become a medal sport in 1992 at the Summer Olympics in Barcelona (baseball was merely a "demonstration" sport at the two previous Olympics), the Russians don't want to be left out. So they're busily perfecting their skills on the diamond, but not in an all-out manner up to this point.

The Soviet's top baseball team currently is the D. I. Mendeleyev Institute of Technology nine which has been competing against collegiate teams on an international basis for the past two or three years.

But, so far, the Mendeleyev squad hasn't met with a great deal of success. For example, the Johns Hopkins University varsity nine traveled to Moscow in the spring of 1988 to play Mendeleyev in a three-game series, with the Americans winning all three contests by lopsided scores of 15–1, 15–2 and 20–3. Did the Russians want revenge?

Yes. Mendeleyev Institute came to the United States in the early fall of 1988, and clashed again with Johns Hopkins in a three-game set. In the opener the Russians were trounced 16–0 as they failed to get a single base hit and committed 6 errors in the first inning alone. Mendeleyev went on—they dropped the other two games by wide margins to Johns Hopkins.

The Mendeleyev Institute of Technology team, made up of players ranging in age from 18 to 31, hopes to sharpen its skills to the point where it can compete successfully at Barcelona in 1992. Thus far, no one has attached an official nickname to the Soviet baseball team, but the label "Men" seems to have been catching on.

David Falkner, *The New York Times* sportswriter, who has seen the Mendeleyev nine in action against Johns Hopkins, says that the "Men" began learning the rudiments of baseball in a rather haphazard way: "At first the Mendeleyevs played with crude or makeshift pieces of equipment (lacrosse balls were sometimes used, and waterlogged balls were continued in play) on grass fields with no markings. Finally, Rick Spooner, who had once played high school baseball in the United States, volunteered to help them. He has been with them ever since."

Spooner provided the Men with videocassettes of U.S. big league games and took them to see several regular New York Mets games at Shea Stadium when they were on the visit to America.

Vadim Kulakov, the Men's 22-year-old catcher, was particularly impressed with Gary Carter's style of play behind the plate and he now wears No. 8 on the back of his jersey, after his hero. Kulakov even curled his very thick, straight hair in Gary Carter style. Some of the Mendeleyev players even suggested that they adopt "Mets" as their official nickname.

After watching the Men in action several times, Falkner concluded that "the usual *sturmovschina* (Russian for taking something over by storm and perfecting it, like basketball or hockey) has not taken place with baseball, at least not so far."

There are only three or four dozen club teams in Russia, and if the Mendeleyevs are the best, the Soviets have a long way to go before they become an international force in baseball.

Chewing Tobacco, Anyone?

Over the years the Japanese professional teams have played well publicized exhibition series with American All-Star squads, and have often trained in the spring with U.S. big-leaguers in Florida and Arizona. And, in the process, young impressionable Japanese players have tried to emulate the American diamond stars in almost every conceivable way.

For example, catchers try to take command of games like a Johnny Bench or a Gary Carter, runners try to slide headfirst like a Pete Rose, and outfielders try to make nonchalant one-handed catches like a Rickey Henderson or a Darryl Strawberry.

They've even tried chewing tobacco like a Nellie Fox, a George Brett, or a Lenny Dykstra. But the Japanese soon gave up stuffing tobacco into their cheeks when they turned a deep green and became sick.

At the moment, there is not a single professional Japanese ballplayer who is a tobacco chewer.

Unfortunately, however, American professionals who play in the Japanese leagues have their own problems in getting enough chaw to get them through the season.

For example, Gene Martin, a hard-hitting ex-major league outfielder, who played for years for Nagoya's Chunichi Dragons of the Central League in Japan, said the toughest problem for him playing in the Far East was keeping supplied with chewing tobacco. He recalled: "I always took a couple of cases with me before the start of each season, and when I ran out, I had to look around for an Army PX that kept the stuff in stock. I never saw a store anywhere in Japan that carried chewing tobacco."

Martin went on to say: "Several times I tried to interest my Japanese teammates in sampling a wad of chaw, but they always recoiled as if I was throwing a cobra at them."

Los Angeles Dodgers Raise Oranges

Walter O'Malley and Branch Rickey, the two major-domos of the Brooklyn Dodgers at the end of World War II, decided to establish their own spring training complex in Florida and picked Vero Beach as the locale where they built Dodgertown, a project completed in 1948.

The Dodgers, who were intensely interested in signing stars from the Negro professional leagues, knew full well that many Florida hotels maintained a strict "No Blacks" policy at the time and to solve that problem they built their own motel-type apartments right at Dodgertown, a facility covering some 450 acres.

After they had built the Dodgertown ballpark (called Holman Stadium), plus adjunct fields, an administration building and the apartments, O'Malley and Rickey discovered that they still had 70 acres left over—and prime farmland at that. So, they proceeded to consign the surplus acreage to a citrus orchard, and they planted and began to grow oranges, as well as grapefruit and lemons, for commercial marketing. And after more than 40 years, the citrus grove is still being operated for profit.

At Least Somebody Came Out to the Ballgame!

It was a cool, gray and drizzly day in Oakland on November 8, 1905 and the long 200-game Pacific Coast League season was grinding to a close, a season that had commenced in mid-March.

The Portland Beavers were in town to clash with the Oakland Oaks and, since both teams were well out of the pennant race, interest in the game was minimal. Nevertheless, the teams' owners were both surprised and chagrined when the paid attendance for the contest came out to a total of *one*, the lowest recorded attendance figure in U.S. professional baseball history.

The fan's name has been lost in the mists of antiquity, but he should be revered as having prevented the Portland-Oakland game from being played in complete privacy.

° **8** °

CARDS AND AUTOGRAPHS

DiMaggio, the "Human Signing Machine"

In recent years, Joe DiMaggio has been one of the popular attractions on the baseball "card show" circuit. Briefly defined, a card show is a baseball memorabilia convention where a variety of dealers offer their wares and where baseball stars—past and present—show up at specified times for autograph sessions. Run-of-the-mill players charge $4 or so per autograph. (Fans have to bring their own materials to be signed: autograph books, photos, baseballs, bats, etc.)

DiMaggio, voted "baseball's greatest living ex-player" ("At my age, I'm glad to be a living ex-anything"), has the highest going autograph rate, $15 a crack.

Joe played a starring role at the "Cincinnati Classic Baseball Card, Memorabilia and Collectibles" show staged to coincide with the All-Star Game played on the second Tuesday of July 1988 at Cincinnati's Riverfront Stadium. During the course of two four-plus-hour sessions, Joe D signed 2,000 times! Veteran major league scout Ed Liberatore, a longtime friend of DiMaggio's, commented on these marathon autograph sessions: "That Joe DiMaggio is a human signing machine. No matter how many autographs he does in a day, his signature is always strong and bold."

Show promoters place a 10-signature per person limit, but there were still a number of staunch DiMaggio fans who were willing to fork over $15 each for 10 autographs. And no checks or credit cards, please. Just good old-fashioned cash!

Yes, there have been numerous complaints from baseball autograph addicts around the country that DiMaggio is charging a bit much for his moniker. In fact, the term "Yankee Clipper" started to be used in derision. What was Joe D's answer to all this criticism? Why, he simply raised the price to $18 and the lines forming at his autograph sessions are just as long as ever!

Duke Snider Would Rather Sign a Thousand Baseballs

"Do you ever get writer's cramp?" we asked Duke Snider at a recent baseball "card show" staged in New York City. Snider, who was appearing at two five-hour sessions, and signing an estimated 2,000 autographs, answered our question without a moment's hesitation:

"Well, I'd much rather sign a thousand baseballs than face Juan Marichal once. Marichal was absolutely the toughest pitcher I ever faced."

Marichal, who spent most of his 16-year big league career, 1960–75, with the San Francisco Giants, piled up a 243–142 lifetime record with a skinny 2.89 ERA.

"And I'd much rather sign autographs at $7 or $8 a crack than carry mail out of the Brooklyn Post Office at $3 or $4 an hour as I did in the off-season during my early years with the Dodgers in the late '40s and early '50s," Snider added.

He went on to say: "Baseball salaries—even for top players—weren't all that high a generation ago, and the chances for making extra money for personal appearances and that sort of thing were practically nil for most of my active career."

Nowadays Snider is obviously making up for lost time. When his autobiography, *The Duke of Flatbush*, came out in the early summer of 1988, his publisher scheduled an appearance for him at a midtown Manhattan bookshop. The lines of people waiting to buy copies of the Duke's autographed book stretched around the entire block!

"Don't Worry, Mom, Your Kids Are with George Brett"

It's 11:30 in the evening immediately following the 1978 All-Star Game, and the scene is the main lobby of San Diego's Sheraton Harbor Island Hotel, headquarters for both the American and National League teams. George Brett, Kansas City Royals' third baseman, emerges from one of the elevators and heads for the registration desk to check out. Tommy Lasorda, winning manager for the National League, spots Brett, goes over to him, pats him on the back, and congratulates him for the excellent game he played. The two men talk baseball for ten minutes or so—and Brett is obviously well taken with Lasorda's outgoing and amiable manner.

It's now close to 11:45 and Brett askes a bellman to call him a cab so he can get to the airport to catch a plane to a distant city where he will rejoin his Royals teammates to begin the season's second half of play. For George Brett it's been a long hard day, and he's clearly a tired young man.

At this point ten boys, ranging in age from about 10 to 12, all wearing Little League baseball uniforms and carrying boxes of baseball bubblegum cards, sidle up to the weary All-Star and plead almost in unison, "Mr. Brett, may we have your autograph?" And they thrust at him cards printed with his color photo.

What will the frazzled Brett do . . . sign or not sign?

Without a moment's hesitation the Royals' young star puts down his suitcase and heavy equipment bag, smiles broadly, signs autographs for every one of the wide-eyed youngsters and finally climbs into his cab. As the taxi speeds off into the darkness, the Little Leaguers chatter happily among themselves.

That gesture is as important a contribution to the All-Star Game and big league baseball as Brett's two hits against National League pitching.

CHARLES (LINDY) LINDSTROM

Son of Hall-of-Famer Bats 1.000, Slugs 3.000

Charlie Lindstrom, son of Hall of Fame National League infielder Fred Lindstrom, was called up by the Chicago White Sox from their Davenport, Iowa, farm club in the Class B Three-I League late in the 1958 season. Lindstrom, 22, a catcher in his second year of pro ball, had done well at Davenport, batting a solid .276 in 127 games and fielding .983 while handling over 750 chances.

Young Lindstrom got into only one game with the White Sox, but he came through in fine style, batting twice, hitting a long triple and taking a base on balls. He batted in a run and scored once. After this stellar debut performance, Lindstrom never got into another major league game.

16

FRED C. (LINDY) LINDSTROM

Outfielder, Pittsburgh, N. L.

Born in Chicago, Ill., 27 years old, 5 feet, 11 inches tall, weighs 155 pounds. Bats right and throws right. Came to the Giants from Toledo in 1924. Started in as a utility man and finally became their star third baseman until the season of 1931 when he was shifted to the outfield. Has spent nine years in the Majors. Traded to Pittsburgh at end of season.

This is one of a series of 32 pictures of famous athletes numbered from 1 to 32. Return a complete set and receive a league BASEBALL, value $1.00, or return three complete sets and receive a FIELDER'S GLOVE, value $3.00 (state whether left or right handed). Your pictures will be returned with the gifts.

UNITED STATES CARAMEL CO.
East Boston, Mass.

We spoke with Charlie's father, Fred Lindstrom, at a 1978 Shea Stadium Old-Timers Day and asked why his son's big league career was aborted after such an auspicious beginning.

The elder Lindstrom answered: "Well, Charlie was called into military service after that 1958 season, and after he got out, things in general were different and he just drifted away from professional baseball."

Nevertheless, Charlie Lindstrom has his name permanently etched in the major league record books as batting an even 1.000 lifetime with a slugging average of 3.000.

A Fred Lindstrom baseball card produced in 1932 by the United States Carmel Co., East Boston, Massachusetts, was uncovered in mid-1988 by Joshua Evans, an Allentown, Pennsylvania, sports memorabilia dealer. It is thought to be the only specimen extant and Evans has placed a price tag of exactly $1 million on the card.

After several noted sports collectibles dealers said the asking price was far too high, Evans replied: "The Lindstrom card is a one-of-a-kind treasure, like a Rembrandt or Van Gogh that is suddenly discovered in some attic. . . . If you've got the only one, it's priceless."

Evans believes the card was pulled out of production to invalidate some kind of retailer's promotional giveaway in the middle of the Depression ("Collect the whole set and win a bike"). For some unknown reason, Fred Lindstrom's middle name, Charles, was used instead of Fred on the card. The fact that Lindstrom is a member of baseball's Hall of Fame adds additional interest to the card.

Mickey's Rate Goes Up

Mickey Mantle was also a star performer at the show, and his autograph fee was also $15 a crack. And in a brace of only four-plus-hour sessions he pushed himself and signed a couple of thousand times.

Tim Sullivan, Cincinnati *Enquirer* sportswriter and a devout Mickey Mantle fan from boyhood, admitted in one of his columns that he bought a $15 ticket for a single signature, waited in line for an hour and was happy when he finally got up to the table where Mickey signed a photograph for him.

Sullivan said later: "Mantle signs, shakes hands, poses for pictures, but keeps the line moving. It is an autograph factory. It is no place to talk." Sullivan also said, "My moment with 'The Mick' was worth the 15 dollars."

He also mentioned that a sign at Mickey's table read, "Mr. Mantle does not sign bats."

It seems that at one of the big card shows a rather unruly crowd lined up to get the autograph of a diamond superstar, and a couple of fans who had baseball bats with them got into a shoving match and used those bats to help settle the argument. After that very unpleasant incident, most players now refuse to sign bats.

Because Mickey Mantle draws such big lines at card shows, we've heard that he's recently raised his rate to $18 and is thinking of eventually going to $20 per autograph. Inflation has definitely hit the autograph market.

Alvin Dark Says "No"

Sometimes when big league ballplayers leave a park after a tough game, they're crotchety and can be even downright mean to youngsters who come chasing after them for autographs. Unfortunately, the kid who gets rejected in cases like this may eventually get his revenge on the hero who scorned him.

For example: After a particularly tough game at the Polo Grounds played during the searing heat of an August afternoon in the 1950 season, Alvin "Blackie" Dark, the star New York Giants shortstop, began leaving the park with the intention of getting home in the quickest possible time.

At the exit gate, however, a brash youngster of about 11 waved his autograph book at Dark and begged "Blackie" to sign it for him.

As Dark looked with disdain at the boy, he muttered through his teeth, "Take a hike, kid, take a hike."

The 11-year-old, disconsolate, trudged away, deeply humiliated.

That boy, named Jim Bouton, grew up to become an ace pitcher for the New York Yankees in the 1960s, and once his playing career drew to a close he took to authorship and wrote the 1970 best seller, *Ball Four*.

In *Ball Four*, Bouton castigated Alvin Dark for his rudeness on that long ago afternoon, and as we read Bouton's words, we could sense that his feelings were still bruised over the incident. Bouton finally had his chance for revenge.

The morale of this tale might be: Look, all you bigtime ballplayers out there: If a kid comes up to you asking for an autograph, sign it for him, no matter how pooped you are. You never know how that insignificant-looking little kid with the autograph book is going to turn out. He may well become another Jim Bouton and really zap you when he grows up!

Gorbachev Says "Yes"

Joe DiMaggio was among the honored guests invited to meet Soviet leader Mikhail Gorbachev at an informal reception and dinner held at the White House in Washington, D.C. back in December 1987. Never one to pass up a good opportunity, the "Yankee Clipper" asked if Gorbachev would autograph a baseball that DiMaggio just happened to have with him. DiMaggio later gave this major league baseball—believed to be the only one in existence signed by Gorbachev—to his friend Barry Halper, an avid collector of baseball memorabilia.

Halper, a New Jerseyite, has added this ball to his collection, which includes more than a million different baseball cards, over a thousand bats, nearly 4,000 autographed baseballs—he has balls signed by every United States president since Woodrow Wilson—and about 900 uniform jerseys.

A minority stockholder in the New York Yankees, Halper later admitted that he's the one who prompted Joe DiMaggio to corner Mikhail Gorbachev for the autograph.

Halper for the past several years has been trying to track down a baseball signed by Abraham Lincoln. "The ball does exist," Halper maintains, "but the collector who has it now just won't sell it to me . . . still, I keep on trying."

Soldiers from the Union Army played baseball during their breaks from fighting, and apparently Lincoln signed a ball while visiting an army camp in Maryland.

Memorabilia Prices on the Rise

A set of two number 9's from the backs of the uniforms worn by Roger Maris when he hit home runs numbers 60 and 61 in 1961 were sold for $4,950 at an October 12, 1988 telephone-bid auction in Allentown, Pennsylvania.

An employee of a New York City company that handled the cleaning and restoration of Yankee uniforms recognized the historical importance of the Maris homers, and so he removed the number 9's from the backs of the jerseys when they came in for cleaning. He attached, of course, new numbers onto the uniforms before they were sent back to the field. More than a quarter-century later, the pair of number 9's found their way into a sports memorabilia auction.

This was the highest auction price ever realized for a *piece* of a baseball uniform, though complete Babe Ruth Boston Red Sox and New York Yankees jerseys have commanded prices of more than $20,000 each.

Roster

A

Aaron, Hank, 102
Alexander, Grover
    Cleveland, 67
Allen, Ethan, 104, 106
Allen, Mel, 58–59, 79–80
Alston, Walter, 33, 69
Altman, George, 31–32
Anderson, George
    (Sparky), 106
Arlett, Russell (Buzz),
    57–58
Averill, Earl, 74

B

Backman, Wally, 21
Banks, Ernie, 101
Bench, Johnny, 111
Bing, Rudolf, 60
Blades, Ray, 67
Bonham, Ernie (Tiny), 15
Bottomley, Jim, 67
Boudreau, Lou, 25, 39,
    42–44
Bouton, Jim, 121
Bradley, Alva, 42
Breen, Gerard, 106
Brett, George, 111, 116
Brock, Lou, 45
Brown, Jim, 50
Brown, Joe (Poison), 67

Buckner, Bill, 21–22
Busch, August A., Jr., 102
Bush, Bucky, 103
Bush, Dorothy Walker, 103
Bush, Nancy Ellis, 103
Bush, President George
    Herbert Walker,
    103–08
Bush, Prescott, Jr., 103
Bush, Senator Prescott, 103

C

Campanella, Roy, 33
Carrasquel, Chico, 77
Carter, Gary, 21, 110, 111
Casey, Hugh, 15–17
Cedeno, Cesar, 75
Clemens, Roger, 75
Cobb, Ty, 45, 84
Coffman, Dick, 93
Collins, James (Rip), 67
Conlan, John Bertrand
    (Jocko), 28–30
Connolly, Tom, 30
Cousins, Norman, 79
Crandall, Del, 101
Cronin, Joe, 93, 98
Crowther, Bosley, 76

D

Dailey, Dan, 76
Dark, Alvin, 121